THE PRINCIPAL AS STAFF DEVELOPER

THE
PRINCIPAL
AS
STAFF DEVELOPER

Richard P. DuFour

NATIONAL EDUCATIONAL SERVICE
BLOOMINGTON, INDIANA · 1991

Cover design by Joe LaMantia

Edited by Dennis Sparks

Printed in the United States of America

Printed on recycled paper

ISBN 1-879639-01-7

TO MATTHEW

Table of Contents

Acknowledgements

My thanks go first to Dennis Sparks, whose interest in and enthusiasm for this work never waned from inception to publication. I remain grateful to the wonderful men and women of Stevenson High School in Prairie View, Illinois. They have created a climate and culture characterized by professionalism, collaboration, and experimentation and serve as models for many of the ideas contained in this book. Finally, I am indebted to Susan and Matthew for their patience and understanding when my attention to this book resulted in inattention to a wonderful wife and son.

— Richard P. DuFour

THE PRINCIPAL AS STAFF DEVELOPER

1

School Improvement
Means People Improvement

The only way we're going to get from where we are to where we want to be is through staff development . . . When you talk about school improvement, you're talking about people improvement. That's the only way to improve schools.

— Ernest Boyer (in Sparks, 1984, p. 35)

Conditions necessary for improvement are motivated primarily by the principal . . . The principal is the critical person in making change happen.

— Anne Lieberman and Lynne Miller (1981, p. 585)

In 1983, the National Commission on Excellence in Education declared that the United States was "at risk" due to a rising tide of mediocrity in public education. The Commission called upon state and local officials to initiate and lead the reforms necessary to restore standards and quality to the schools of the nation. Within two years of its report, over three hundred national and state task forces had investigated the condition of public schooling in America. In 41 states, legislatures had shown their support for excellence in education by mandating that students take more courses in designated academic areas. In many states, requirements for teacher certification and tenure had been raised, and steps had been taken to standardize curriculum and mandate testing.

The United States Department of Education (1984) described this response to *A Nation at Risk* as "nothing short of extraordinary" (p. 11). Only twelve months after the Commission on Excellence had made its pronouncements on the critical state of American education, Secretary of Education Terrell Bell (1984) reported with satisfaction that the arduous work of reform was "already bearing fruit" (p. 8).

However, on the fifth anniversary of the publication of *A Nation of Risk,* the Department of Education acknowledged that the "excellence" initiative had failed to transform the schools. As Secretary of Education William Bennett glumly reported, "We are still at risk" (Ordovensky, A3). At this juncture, it should be more apparent than ever that the best hope of genuine, significant school improvement lies not in state mandates or manipulation of graduation requirements, but in the development of the full potential of the professional staffs within our schools. This book is intended to convey both the critical significance of staff development in a school-improvement effort and the importance of the principal in determining the success of a staff development program. The assumptions which underlie this book are that:

1. *The local school district and school provide the best arena for school improvement efforts.* The focus of educational reform efforts must be the individual school. There are many things that state legislatures can mandate — teacher certification requirements, minimum days of school attendance, and even subjects to be taught. However, a legislature cannot mandate a commitment to excellence or even to school improvement in a local school district. Mandates inevitably deal with minimums, with lowest common denominators. The energy and effort needed to improve a school cannot be sustained by such minimums. The commitment to improvement must come from within: it cannot be imposed. Furthermore, the improvement of education depends on decisions and actions at the school site. It is the local school that is in the best position to create a vision of what it seeks to become, to assess areas which must be improved, and to develop the strategies and programs to make those improvements (Levine and Lezotte, 1990). As John Gardner (1988) observed, state education officials who are trying to "suck up all the authority to the state level are acting one hundred eighty degrees opposite" (p. 75) to what is in the best interests of school improvement. A structure more conducive to reform is the concept of reasonably autonomous schools linked both to a hub (the central office) and to each other in a network (Goodlad, 1984). Substantial decision-making authority at the school site is an essential prerequisite for quality education (*Ventures,* 1985). Thus, the best bet for improving schools lies not in fine-tuning

state reforms, but in stimulating individual school districts and schools to change and providing them with the resources and time to do it.

2. *School improvement means people improvement.* It has been charged that a major thrust of the excellence movement has been an effort to "teacher-proof" the schools. An underlying assumption of the movement seems to have been that someone other than teachers—state legislatures, consultants, textbook publishers, etc.—should determine the curriculum to be taught, the instructional strategies to be used, the pace to be followed, the acceptable materials to be utilized, and the assessment instruments to be monitored. Ironically, the movement's emphasis on regulations and controls stands in direct contrast to the strategy of providing greater individual autonomy which has been found to be most effective in other organizations. While the corporate world has recognized the importance of the individual worker, education seems bent on trying to fix the system from the top. The "excellence movement" has typically failed to recognize teachers as professionals and has denied them the autonomy essential to effective teaching. It should be self-evident that the quality of personnel is of central importance to a school, and that enabling individuals to improve their effectiveness is the key to any meaningful school improvement effort. Boyer (in Sparks, 1984) stated the position most eloquently:

The only way we are going to get from where we are to where we want to be is through staff development. When you talk about school improvement, you're talking about people improvement. That's the only way to improve schools unless you mean painting the buildings and fixing the floors. But that's not the school, that's the shell. The school is people, so when we talk about excellence or improvement or progress, we're really talking about the people who make up the building (p. 9).

Often, schools attempt to present programs dealing with the peripheral issues of education as meaningful school improvement. New curriculum materials, alternative scheduling arrangements, or higher school-wide grading scales are heralded as examples of school improvement. Such posturing brings to mind the novice golfer who continually seeks to find the ultimate secret of golf success in purchasing new and improved clubs, balls, or shoes rather than in developing the mechanics of his game. School improvement is not new programs and packages. Procedures and materials do not bring about change — people do. School districts typically devote the greatest portion of their revenue to personnel, and it only makes sense that the development of this human resource must be at the very heart of a school improvement effort. Excellence in education will be achieved only if schools invest in the training and development of their professional staffs.

3. *The principal is a key figure in determining the ultimate success of any effort to develop school personnel and thus plays a major role in school improvement.* Principals play the key role in creating the conditions which result in more effective schools. In his study of selected high schools, Boyer (1983) found that, in schools with high achievement and a clear sense of community, it was invariably the principal that made the difference, a finding consistently supported by the research on effective schools.

Studies of the school improvement process also reinforce the critical role of the principal in that process. One synthesis of research on effective schools concluded that the conditions necessary for improvement are motivated primarily by the principal (Lieberman and Miller, 1981). A study of hundreds of federally funded, innovative educational programs led to the conclusion that one of the major factors affecting the ultimate success of the program was the support of the principal (Berman and McLaughlin, 1978). Conversely, Goodlad (1984) charged that the primary reason most schools are unable to solve school-wide problems is because the principal lacks the requisite skills of group leadership. For better or for worse, principals are in the pivotal position in school improvement.

Given the importance of the principal in determining both the effectiveness of a school and the success of a school-improvement effort, it is not surprising that the principal has also been found to play the major role in determining the ultimate value of a staff development program (The Center for Educational Policy and Management, 1985). Principals typically function as gatekeepers for change and innovation, and the eventual outcome of a staff development initiative often rests upon the guidance and support furnished by the principal (Wood, Thompson and Russell, 1981). Again and again, the commitment and support of the principal is described as essential to successful staff development programs. As a report of the American Association of School Administrators (1986) summarized:

What is most likely to underpin the success of a district's staff development program—variety and richness of offerings, skill in which seminars are conducted, fame and fire of teacher trainers? It is the principal who tips the scale toward an effective staff development program (p. 31).

In light of these findings, it is distressing that principals have often limited their involvement in staff development programs to arranging for speakers at disjointed inservice programs. Too often, principals have looked upon staff development as a secondary consideration, an aspect of the operation of the school which warranted little, if any, of their time and attention. In fact, the principal as staff developer is an integral part of the concept of the principal as instructional leader. One of the very best indicators of instructional leadership is the presence of an ongoing, school-based staff development program and a school climate in which that program can flourish. Teacher perceptions support this research finding. Teachers who regard their principals as strong instructional leaders invariably point to the principal's active involvement in staff development activities as evidence of instructional leadership (Smith and Andrews, 1990). Principals who wish to fulfill the role of instructional leaders must recognize their responsibilities in the development of the staffs they are attempting to lead. They must assume an active part in staff development if meaningful school improvement is to take place.

4. *Schools seeking meaningful improvement must make a commitment to staff development programs that are purposeful and goal-directed.* Although staff development is generally recognized as the training of personnel, various authors have given the term different emphasis. This book regards staff development as "the deliberate effort to alter the professional practices, beliefs and understandings of school personnel toward an articulated end" (Fielding and Schalock, 1985, p. 14). This latter definition emphasizes the intentional, purposeful, goal-directed professional development which this book promotes. A staff development program should represent the means to an end rather than the end itself. The goal is not merely to provide a program but to provide a program that will enhance the effectiveness of a school and its staff.

Too often, staff development programs have subjected teachers to an occasional day-long workshop conducted by "experts on leave from Mt. Olympus" who were "long on process, short on substance and knew little about the classroom" (Boyer, 1983, p. 179). Sparks (1987) found that teachers typically regard their inservice training as "useless, one-shot dog and pony shows" (p. 17) that had little real influence on their competence. An extensive study of schooling practices across the nation found that staff development programs are generally fragmented and unfocused with no clear setting of priorities or in-depth attacks on schoolwide problems (Goodlad, 1984).

This haphazard approach to the development of human assets stands in marked contrast to the practice of leading businesses and industries. *Business Week* (1986) described the inservice training of employees as "one of the fastest growing industries in the business world today" (p. 340). The total corporate investment in company and business education was estimated at $40 billion each year, and Harold Hodgkins calculated that the value of on-the-job training in industry approximates the net worth of the 3,500 colleges and universities in the United States (Elam, Cramer and Brodinsky, 1986). AT&T alone spent $1.7 billion on employee training in 1980, and IBM, which spent nearly $700 million in 1984, requires all managers to undergo ninety hours of training each year (Lewis, 1986). These companies have acknowledged the benefits of ongoing training that allows their human assets to appreciate. It is time that education, one of this nation's most labor-intensive endeavors, is approached from a similar standpoint.

Although the financial conditions of most school districts will not allow them to devote as significant a proportion of their budgets to personnel development as the private sector, the programs that are developed can be more effectively designed to help the district achieve its goals. In recent years, research has provided a clearer picture of the components of effective staff development. This book describes the essential characteristics of quality staff development programs and the role that principals can play in promoting such programs.

2

The Principal as Leader

We are finally learning that leadership is all about getting people engaged, involved, committed and excited about a useful vision that is about quality and innovation . . . Running a great secondary school has precisely the same elements.

—Tom Peters (1988, p. 39)

Unless the leader knows where the whole venture is headed, it will not be possible to carry out the other tasks of leadership.

—John Gardner (1988, p. 6)

LEADERSHIP is often confused with position and power. There are undoubtedly men and women who assume that they are the instructional leaders of their schools because they hold the position of principal or have the power to evaluate programs and personnel. However, the fact that the principalship is placed above the position of teacher on the traditional hierarchy of the organizational chart insures the principal only of subordinates, not of followers. Nor does the fact that an individual completes some of the tasks associated with the principalship — scheduling, providing an orderly climate, allocating resources to programs, etc. — necessarily mean that the person is functioning as instructional leader. In their study of leaders from a number of different walks of life, Warren Bennis and Burt Nanus (1985) drew a distinction between managers and leaders by suggesting that, while "managers are people who do things right . . . leaders are people who do the right things" (p. 21). What, then, is leadership, and what are the "right things" for principals to do if they hope to function as instructional leaders?

THE IMPORTANCE OF VISION

Leadership is the process of persuasion and example by which an individual attempts to influence a group to take action that is in accord with the leader's purpose or the shared purpose of all. James McGregor Burns (1978) advised that the first thing a leader must do in an effort to influence others is to clarify his or her own goals. Bennis and Nanus (1985) described this purposefulness and clarity of goals as "vision — a view of a realistic, credible, attractive future for the organization, a condition that is better in some important ways than what now exists" (p. 89). In fact, the importance of vision has been cited so frequently in the research on leaders, organizations, and schools that it must be considered an essential prerequisite of leadership. It is simply not possible to carry out the other tasks of leadership unless the leader has a clear sense of where the organization is going and how it is going to get there.

This generalization holds true for principals who hope to serve as effective instructional leaders. One of the most important acts of leadership they can provide is to help teachers and parents develop a widely supported, compelling vision of the school they would like to create. Consider the following statements:

In an effective school the principal has a clear vision of where the school is going and communicates it to staff, students and parents (Northwest Regional Educational Laboratory, 1984, p. 7).

Effective principals have a sense of vision as to the kind of school and learning environment they intend to create. They articulate goals, directions, and priorities for their schools (Cawelti, 1984, p. 3).

Instructional leaders have a clear vision of what the school is trying to accomplish . . . Out of this sense of mission evolves a sense of purpose shared by the staff, students, and community (Hollinger and Murphy, 1987, p. 57).

A key characteristic of a successful school leader is [the ability] to create an exciting vision about what an institution can be . . . It's the ability to paint a picture, to describe an attractive future that gets other people turned on (Peters, 1988, p. 37).

The real challenge today for principals is establishing a vision of what a healthy school is and embedding it in the minds of faculty, parents and community (Gardner, 1988, pp. 76-77).

If staff development is indeed "the deliberate effort to alter the professional practices, beliefs and understandings of school persons toward an articulated end" (Fielding and Schalock, 1985, p. 14), as suggested in Chapter One, it should be evident that a principal who is unable to define that "end" is also unable to develop the programs and policies to get there. There is simply no question that it is easier to move a school from Point A to Point B if the principal and staff know where Point B is located and how to recognize it once they arrive. Thus, the very first step that principals must take if they hope to fulfill their responsibilities as staff developers is to provide leadership in formulating and articulating a vision of the future for their schools.

REACHING CONSENSUS ON VISION

Although principals should have strong convictions regarding the qualities and conditions they hope to promote within their schools, they should not attempt to develop a vision for their schools unilaterally. Education is very much a collective endeavor, and commitment to a particular vision cannot be obtained through edict or coercion. Bennis and Nanus (1985) found that, while effective leaders articulated a vision, gave it form and legitimacy and focused attention upon it, they rarely were the ones who conceived of the vision in the first place. In order for a vision to guide and motivate the people within an organization, it must grow out of their needs, hopes, and dreams. The members of the organization who will be asked to embrace and "own" the vision should play a role in drafting it. One of the most important acts of leadership an individual can provide within an organization is to oversee a process which both allows for this participation and results in a vision that has widespread support throughout the organization. In fact, the ability

of the principal to gain general support for the vision
which is to direct the school plays a critical role in determining the eventual success of a school improvement
effort. As Levine and Lezotte (1990) found in their study
of unusually effective schools:

Currently we see all too many principals trying to "do it alone"
. . . It is unlikely that widespread school improvement can be
successfully begun, let alone sustained, without a broad-based
empowerment of all those who are stakeholders in the culture
of the school. When we find successful examples of groups of
schools that are changing, we generally see widespread
"ownership" of both the mission and strategies for change
(p. 71).

The process that principals might utilize to develop a
widely supported sense of direction and purpose can
range from the simple and informal to the complex and
highly structured. Robert Waterman (1987) suggested
that an effective method for developing a useful vision
statement is simply to hold a series of discussions in which
members of the organization are asked to share their
thoughts on four key questions. Applied to the school
setting, these questions are:

1. Looking back on the history of our school, what
have we done that gives us the most pride?
2. Looking back, of what ought we to be ashamed?
3. What could we do now that would make us proud?
4. Ten years from now, looking back at what we have
done, what will make us proud?   (p. 242)

Bill Cook (1988), an advocate of strategic planning for
school districts, offered a lengthier, more formal approach
to setting direction and goals that is easily adaptable to an
individual school. This strategic planning process calls for
the formulation of a planning team of twenty to twenty-

five members who are selected from a pool of volunteers on the basis of several considerations. First, the team is to include both those who have responsibility for establishing overall direction, policies, and objectives as well as those who are responsible for the implementation of policy. Second, the team must represent every component of the school—building administrators, certified staff, classified staff, teachers' union, community leaders, parents, and students. Third, members of the committee should be persons of good will who are willing to pursue consensus. The planning team begins the process by developing a statement of the beliefs, convictions, or fundamental values that should guide the school. From this statement of beliefs comes a clear, one-sentence mission statement which provides an expression of the school's purpose and function. The mission statement reflects the vision of what the school is striving to become. Based upon this statement, the planning team develops policies, assesses strengths and weaknesses, reviews significant factors external to the organization, identifies critical issues, develops statements of objectives in specific, measurable terms, and lists general strategies to accomplish the objectives. At this point in the process, additional committees are formed to develop action plans —detailed descriptions of the specific actions required to achieve the results called for in the objectives. The action planning teams also develop cost–benefit analyses for their plans and report their recommendations to the planning committee for review and approval.

A high school in suburban Chicago used an approach which combined aspects of the different procedures recommended by Waterman and Cook. A task force of fifteen members was convened to help draft a vision statement for the school. Members were invited by the principal to serve on the task force, seeking to have representation for each of the affected school groups—

administrators, teachers, parents, students, community leaders, and business representatives. Members were selected on the basis of their respect and influence within their constituent group, as well as for their ability to see the "big picture" and seek compromise. In its initial meeting, the principal led the task force in a review of its purpose and parameters and shared a summary of the research on effective schools. The task force was then given the charge to determine the community's concept of an "excellent school" and draft a description of a school which reflected that concept. For several months, members of the task force led discussions throughout the school and community, based upon a single question: "What do you believe are the characteristics of an excellent school?" Student leaders surveyed classmates in homerooms. Teachers led discussions in small-group meetings of faculty. Parents posed the question at PTA meetings and to a variety of parent booster groups. Community members presented the topic at church meetings, Rotary luncheons, and sessions of the Chamber of Commerce. The members of the task force then reconvened to share their findings and to begin the task of looking for characteristics that had been cited by all or most of the different groups. From this list of common characteristics the committee drafted an extensive narrative describing an excellent school. A draft of this narrative was shared with each of the groups who had participated in the initial discussions, and feedback was solicited. Revisions were then made by the task force on the basis of this feedback. Finally, the description of an excellent school was submitted to the Board of Education, which adopted the description as Board policy and directed the administration to develop policies and procedures to move the school toward that ideal (DuFour and Eaker, 1987).

Yet another model that calls for both the development

of a vision statement and the programs to promote that vision is an eleven-module inservice program (Brookover, et al., 1982) based upon the findings of the research on effective schools. The first step in this model is the development of a school mission statement which sets forth the purpose of the school and the fundamental beliefs which guide its policies and programs. The faculty and principal play the major role in the drafting of this statement.

Whereas there is considerable flexibility regarding the model that principals might use to develop vision statements for their schools, the critical importance of arriving at this common understanding as to what a school stands for and what it is attempting to become cannot be over-emphasized. Yogi Berra's observation, "If you don't know where you are going, you probably aren't going to get there," should be posted in the office of every principal as a reminder of the importance of clear vision. Principals should see to it that their schools have a vision statement that is written, highly publicized, widely supported, and constantly utilized as a guide in the development of programs and policies to advance their schools.

SHARED VALUES — THE MEANS TO AN END

If vision is a target that beckons, values are the behaviors and attitudes that are necessary to move a school toward that target. They carry the messages of shared purpose, shared standards, and shared conceptions of what is worth working for. The importance of explicit, shared values has been cited repeatedly in studies of effective organizations and leaders. In his work on leadership, Gardner (1986B) concluded that, unless there is a base of shared values among constituents, leaders cannot function effectively. Peters and Waterman (1983) found the attention to shaping values so prevalent in the companies they studied that they questioned whether it was possible for an organization to be excellent without having the right values and a clear understanding of those values. Sergiovanni (1984) concluded that this attention to shaping values was also a critical element in creating excellent schools. Deal and Peterson (1990) found that a clear and focused sense of values was the critical common factor among the succesful principals whom they studied. Thus, the extent to which a principal can use a vision statement to influence a school depends in large part upon the degree to which that vision is reflected in the explicit core values that are recognized within the school and promoted on a day-to-day basis.

Whereas the vision statement reflects the end toward which the school is striving, the values represent the means which are necessary to achieve that end. For example, the vision statement of a school might include, "This school is committed to the goal of helping *all* students achieve the intended instructional outcomes of the district." The essential question then becomes, what teacher behaviors and attitudes must be in evidence if that vision is to become a reality? A staff might conclude that the following values are necessary:

1. We will identify the specific outcomes that students are to achieve on a course-by-course basis.

2. We will teach to the agreed-upon outcomes and accept our responsibility to help each student achieve those outcomes.

3. We will monitor each student's attainment of outcomes on an ongoing basis and adjust our instructional strategies accordingly.

Thus, once a school has completed its process for developing a vision statement, the faculty should go through a similar process to specify the values — behaviors and attitudes — they will promote to advance toward that vision. This important step in the improvement process should not be overlooked.

Two important considerations should guide the development of a list of values for a school. First, the list should be brief; the longer the litany of "thou shalts," the less likely it is to be remembered by teachers, and thus the less likely it is to be effective in guiding them. Second, the statements should be sufficiently specific to give direction to the daily activities and decisions of the faculty. The fundamental purpose of explicitly stated values is to help promote specific attitudes and behaviors, to give teachers a sense of how things are to be done. Platitudes lack the specificity to serve this purpose.

Once again, the concept of staff development presupposes deliberate efforts to alter the professional practices and beliefs of educators toward an articulated end. Thus it should be apparent that principals must have a clear sense of both vision (the articulated end) and values (the professional practices and beliefs necessary to progress toward those ends) if they are to serve as effective staff developers. Only when principals are clear on vision and values can they hope to be the purposeful change agents that effective staff development requires.

THE PRINCIPAL AS CHANGE AGENT

One of the major benefits of developing a vision statement is the fact that it stimulates change. Once a school has the benefit of a compelling description of what it is trying to become, it is able to compare that description to existing conditions and to develop an agenda to reduce the discrepancies. The contribution to change has been described as the fundamental task of the leadership function. Principals who seek to fulfill this fundamental task must continually struggle to identify the changes that will help the school move closer toward its vision. Principals must recognize and embrace their role as change agents.

One study (Walker and Vogt, 1987) of the skills that principals need to function as effective change agents offered the following list:

1. Intrapersonal skills — knowing one's own motivation and role in change
2. Facilitating the need for change — assessing needs and identifying problems
3. Collaboration — promoting cooperative, collegial relationships
4. Action planning — selecting from among alternatives and setting goals
5. Plan implementation — dealing with resistance and determining responsibilities
6. Evaluation — assessing the results of the change
7. Institutionalization — institutionalizing the change so that its continued existence no longer depends upon the principal

Another study (Fielding and Schalock, 1985) cited seven functions that principals must successfully perform if they are to be effective change agents through staff development:

1. Establish priorities. Staff development plans must be anchored in the long-term improvement goals of the school.
2. Develop designs. Designs for staff development must be matched to the outcomes they are intended to produce as well as to the people who are to participate.
3. Clarify roles and responsibilities. Various participants in the staff development program must be clear about who is responsible for what.

4. Provide support. Participants must be encouraged, have access to both material and human resources, and have sufficient time to bring about change.

5. Monitor progress. Procedures must exist for tracking the progress that participants are making in implementing desired practices and for detecting problems that arise during the course of implementation.

6. Evaluate effects. Assess the impact of the program on teaching and learning.

One point bears re-emphasis: Principals who hope to function as effective change agents should have a clear sense of organizational vision and values (Deal and Peterson, 1990). A synthesis (Lieberman and Miller, 1981) of the research on schools that were improving concluded that clear underlying vision and values provided the "system" which guided their improvement efforts. The leaders of these schools avoided "seat-of-the-pants" management by taking the long view and using vision and values as a map of where to go without limiting the number of ways to get there. Principals who recognize their role as staff developers should not take their first steps on the path to school improvement without having this map firmly in hand.

3

Creating a Climate for Effective Staff Development

A positive school climate is perhaps the single most important expression of educational leadership.

Scott Thomson (1980, p. 11)

Within the context of a limited set of clear goals for students... teachers, working together, must be free to exercise their professional judgment as to how to achieve these goals.

— Carnegie Foundation Forum on
Education and the Economy (1986, p. 58)

VISION AND VALUES ALONE will not ensure the effectiveness of principals as staff developers. It is clear that the seeds of staff development efforts flourish best in certain school climates, and it is up to principals to promote a productive climate within their schools. Students have found *unanimously* that organizational climate is critical to the success of change efforts (Sparks, 1987). Climate, which is sometimes used interchangeably with culture, can be defined as the collective set of attitudes, beliefs, and behaviors within a building that make up the group norm (Brookover, et al., 1979). This norm represents shared expectations for behavior and serves as a guide for what is to be done, how it is to be done, and by whom. Discussions of organizational climate often focus on the degree of satisfaction expressed by the members of the organization. A more valid approach to school climate considers it as a measure of both satisfaction and productivity, which, in the case of schools, can be described as student achievement.

There is widespread agreement that it is the principal who plays the major role in shaping the climate of a school (Brookover, et al., 1979; Kelley, 1980; Lieberman and Miller, 1981). As Edgar Kelley stated simply:

If there is a single tool a principal should have, it is a mirror. Looking in that mirror, the principal can find the person who more than any other is both responsible for and accountable for the feelings of satisfaction and productivity for staff, students and patrons (p. 53).

What are the norms or climatic conditions which seem to promote successful school improvement efforts? A meta-analysis of research on productive school climate (Georgiades, Fuentes and Snyder, 1983) listed the following conditions:

I. PREDISPOSITIONS
   A. Student-centered orientation. Educational decisions are centered on meeting each student's learning needs.
   B. Improvement orientation. Leadership and staff visibly support improvement and the search for new ways.
   C. Success orientation. Staff members have high expectations for students and for each other.

II. COLLABORATIVE WORK BEHAVIOR
   A. Common goal focus. There is school-wide agreement on goals.
   B. Continuous dialogue. There are frequent opportunities to exchange ideas on instruction, student performance, teaching techniques, and problems in general.
   C. Shared decision-making. Leadership solicits, uses, and supports decisions from those charged with implementing and those most affected by the decision.
   D. Planned action. Curriculum, instruction, and testing are carefully planned and co-ordinated.
   E. Periodic reflection and feedback. Progress is carefully monitored. Concrete and specific feedback is given to teachers, and individual achievements are recognized.

III. PROFESSIONAL PRODUCTIVITY
   A. Cognitive. The staff has a strong knowledge base

about instruction and learning principles which is supported with ongoing staff development.

B. Affective. The leader structures opportunities for the staff to feel a part of a cohesive group.

C. Behavioral. The staff is purposeful, involved, and concerned.

The climate described in this analysis and in numerous other studies calls for teachers to be given opportunities for the autonomy, collegial collaboration, and experimentation which foster school improvement. Each of these conditions warrants consideration.

AUTONOMY

Treating teachers as professionals is at the very heart of the issue of creating a school climate conducive to staff development. Professionalism suggests a high level of knowledge and skill, status commensurate with that skill, and, most importantly, the opportunity to exercise one's own judgment. In its report on the working conditions facing most teachers, the Carnegie Forum for Education and the Economy (1986) charged that teachers are rarely afforded the status of professionals. The Forum concluded that the management of schools typically seemed to operate on the assumption that teachers lack the talent or motivation to think for themselves.

Gene Maeroff (1988) described teachers as the "field hands on the plantation with not enough say about the conditions in which they are asked to carry out the teaching and learning mission of the school" (p. 52). Teachers share this perception of their lack of autonomy. A survey ("Teachers," 1986) of over 8,500 teachers revealed that only 28 percent of them could be classified as playing a major role in decision-making. More than 85 percent of the respondents believed that the quality of instruction would improve if they were allowed to increase their involvement in curriculum decisions. Eighty percent said they were never consulted about who gets hired in the school. In another national survey of teachers, the majority of respondents indicated that they were not involved in the decision-making process in eight of the ten areas of schooling included in the survey (Maeroff, 1988). Yet another survey, conducted by the Carnegie Foundation for the Advancement of Teaching, found that teachers had grown even more dispirited by their confrontation with working conditions that left them more responsible but less empowered (Norris, 1988). Boyer (1988) concluded that the profession of teaching in this nation remains imperiled — not because of low salaries or credential standards but because the day-to-day conditions within schools typically leave teachers without the opportunity to make decisions.

The first step which principals must take to break this cycle and create a climate for effective staff development is to empower their teaching staffs. Empowerment has been defined as "the degree to which the opportunity to use power effectively is granted or withheld from individuals" (Kanter, 1983, p. 18). In the school setting, empowerment means holding teachers accountable for results, but also providing them with an environment in which they have the opportunity to act upon their ideas, are treated as professionals, and have the freedom to decide how best to meet state and local goals for children (The Carnegie Forum on Education and the Economy, 1986). Jerry Bellon (1988) provided an excellent explanation of the dynamics of the concept:

Empowerment begins with the belief that all people are capable of taking action to improve their work. The process gets underway when leaders express faith that others can and will meet high expectations. Instead of controlling people, leaders assist people in strengthening skills and developing their best attributes. This affirmation of competence elevates the spirit and status of everyone in the organization. People are more involved in their work as they are included in the decisions that affect their responsibility (pp. 30–31).

The beneficial effects of empowerment upon individual motivation and performance have been acknowledged both within and outside of education. Rosabeth Moss Kanter (1983) found that organizations with a history of successful innovation aroused the desire to act among employees by providing them with the freedom to act. Thomas Peters and Robert Waterman (1983) found that workers who were given the freedom to determine some of their goals and the autonomy to develop the strategies to achieve them consistently out-performed their more rigidly supervised counterparts. An analysis of research on excellent schools concluded that teachers within those schools enjoyed a great deal of freedom and autonomy (Sergiovanni, 1984).

Although the National Association of Secondary School Principals endorsed "substantial de-centralization of decision-making authority" and supported the contention that "enlightened organizations include staff members in decision-making processes" (*Ventures,* p. 6), principals have often demonstrated a reluctance to embrace the concept of empowerment. Various studies of both effective schools and effective principals have consistently painted a picture of strong, aggressive, assertive principals who are quick to seize the initiative.

For many school administrators, the concept of empowerment is difficult to reconcile with this image of instructional leadership. This difficulty, however, is based on a muddled view of both empowerment and leadership. The empowerment of teachers and strong instructional leadership on the part of the principalship are *not* mutually exclusive. Principals who empower their staffs do not simply turn teachers loose, let them go off and do whatever they want, and hope for the best. Instead, they use the core values and the intended curricular outcomes of the school to provide a clear structure which enables teachers to work within established boundaries in creative and autonomous ways. These principals demand rigid adherence to the values at the same time that they encourage innovation and autonomy in day-to-day operations. This management style has been described as "simultaneously loose and tight" (Peters and Waterman, 1983, p. 15) and "directed autonomy" (Waterman, 1987, p. 82). Based upon the belief that those closest to the job are often in the best position to suggest improvements in it, it regards every staff member as a source of creative input.

Schools which follow the dictates of directed autonomy have been characterized as both tightly and loosely coupled. On the one hand, there exists a strong sense of core values which define the parameters of behavior and are vigilantly promoted and protected. On the other hand, teachers are given a great deal of freedom as to how these values are to be realized (Sergiovanni, 1984).

Principals who regard calls for teacher empowerment as a subversive attempt to erode their own power and authority are unlikely to respond favorably to the proposals. However, the real issue which should preoccupy principals is not, "Who is in control?" but rather, "How can we best get results?" Giving teachers an opportunity to exercise their judgment serves two practical and powerful purposes toward this end. First, it promotes greater density of leadership. Vitality in a school depends upon the willingness of a great many people within it to take the initiative in identifying and solving problems. The willingness to assume responsibility is the very essence of leadership. As principals are able to persuade others to assume responsibility, they expand the base of leadership within a school.

Second, empowerment eliminates excuses for failure to perform. People can't blame failure on the decisions of others when they are free to determine how to complete a task. When a group of teachers works together to determine the curriculum of a course and its intended outcomes, the textbooks and materials to be used, the appropriate instructional strategies and pacing, and the best methods of assessing student achievement, it is difficult for those teachers to blame poor results on others. Although principals who empower their teaching staffs may indeed give up a measure of control in some areas, they do so in order to gain greater control over what really matters — results.

COLLABORATION

In his extensive study of schooling practices in the United States, Goodlad (1984) found that teachers rarely had the opportunity to join with their peers in collective endeavors. There were few instances of teachers exchanging ideas or practices, and teachers rarely worked together on schoolwide problems. The isolation of teachers is apparent to anyone who has spent time in the classroom and has frequently been cited in research (Fullan, 1990). Indeed, teaching has been described as the second most private act in which adults engage. This isolation poses a formidable barrier to effective staff development, and thus principals who seek to provide an appropriate climate for staff development must make a conscious effort to make collaboration the norm within their schools (Leithwood, 1990).

Participation in cooperative, collegial groups provides teachers with a forum to publicly test their ideas about teaching and expands their level of expertise by allowing them to hear the new ideas of others (Wildman and Niles, 1987). Group discussion and collective problem-solving generally result in better decisions and increase the likelihood of ownership in the decisions (Dillon-Peterson, 1986). Furthermore, as teachers attempt to develop new skills, collaboration helps to reduce the fear of risk-taking by providing encouragement, moral support, and tolerance for error. Finally, some innovations require teachers working together toward common or complimentary goals if the innovations are to have a significant impact (Fielding and Schalock, 1985).

The use of small teams provides an excellent vehicle for collaboration. Different studies (Naisbitt and Aburdene, 1985; Deal and Kennedy, 1983; Kanter, 1983) have predicted that the use of the small team will characterize organizations of the future. Kanter (1983) found that the small-team concept already plays a major role in our most innovative companies. An analysis of studies assessing the impact of small collegial support groups for teachers concluded that such collaboration resulted in greater student achievement, more positive interpersonal relationships and cohesion as a staff, increased social support within the faculty, and enhanced self-esteem for the educators (Johnson and Johnson, 1987). Whether called task forces, quality circles, problem-solving groups, or shared-responsibility teams, such vehicles for greater participation are an important part of an innovative school.

There are a number of ways in which the small-team concept could be implemented in schools as a means of promoting collaboration. For example:

1. By grade level or subject. All teachers of a particular grade in a building could assume responsibility for carrying out responsibilities such as developing curricular

outcomes, assessing student achievement, selecting instructional materials, planning and presenting staff development programs, participating in peer observation and coaching, developing schedules, and hiring new staff.

2. By similar teaching assignment. All teachers of accelerated or remedial students could work to develop or coordinate expectations, materials, assignments, disciplinary consequences, methods of evaluation, and so on.

3. Interdepartmentally. All teachers of freshman-level courses in the humanities could work to develop particular themes to be emphasized across departments.

4. In school-wide task forces. Small groups of teachers could be formed to consider a particular problem and develop recommendations for resolving it.

5. By area of professional development. Teams of teachers could jointly pursue training in a given area of professional development. For example, teachers interested in applying cooperative learning techniques in their classrooms could meet as a team to react to presentations on the topic, develop strategies for using it in the classroom, share related articles, plan peer observation and feedback sessions, and serve as a support group that discusses and analyzes successes and setbacks in their attempt to use the new technique.

The use of small teams promotes collaborations, helps to build consensus, and allows for the development of the leadership potential of a large number of teachers. Furthermore, it accentuates peer pressure, which has been described as "the single, strongest motivating factor for individuals in this post-industrial era" (Deal and Kennedy, 1982, p. 184). In short, the use of small teams is an excellent means of encouraging the collaboration which fosters a productive climate for effective staff development.

Principals can also promote a spirit of collaboration

through their own dealings with staff members. A study of schools that had successfully implemented improvement programs revealed a close, collaborative working relationship between principals and teachers. Matthew Miles (1983) reported, "It was very clear that an underlying variable we called *teacher–administrator harmony* was critical for success" (p. 19). A summary of research studies (Elam, Cramer and Brodinsky, 1986) advised principals who hope to play a positive role in staff development to consider the following collaborative strategies:

1. Develop partnerships with teachers to work for improved instruction.

2. Work with teachers in identifying classroom problems that call for exploration through inservice.

3. Gear principal–teacher conferences toward problem-solving procedures.

4. Encourage self-improvement for teachers by directing their attention to formal and informal staff development activities.

5. Attend inservice training sessions as partners in learning with teachers.

6. Allow teachers freedom in the classroom to practice techniques learned during inservice training.

7. Do away with the notion that there are required ways to teach and that the principal knows what they are.

8. Solicit teacher ideas in planning short-range and long-range staff development programs.

9. Conduct faculty meetings in such a way that they are, at least in part, learning and self-improvement opportunities.

10. Promote among teachers feelings of professional pride, enhanced self-image, and self-efficacy.

The essential point is this: Collaboration among teachers and between principals and teachers helps to create a healthy environment for staff development. In fact, the major staff development issue confronting schools today is the critical need to replace the isolation and separation of school personnel with new organizational norms which base school improvement efforts upon collegial collaboration (Joyce and Murphy, 1990).

EXPERIMENTATION

Phillip Schlecty (1990) made a compelling argument for experimentation in schools when he observed that, "If schools always do what they have done, they will always get what they have got." Improvement requires some change in existing conditions and thus requires people who are willing to change. The very purpose of staff development is to persuade individuals to approach their responsibilities from a different perspective and/or to attempt to use new techniques and strategies — in short, to experiment. Therefore, a willingness to experiment is an important precondition for successful staff development. In fact, the autonomy and collaboration which comprise the other essential elements of a productive climate for staff development are specifically intended to result in an increased willingness to experiment.

The willingness of teachers to experiment — to put forth the effort and energy required to attempt a new approach or technique — depends to a great extent upon their sense of self-confidence and belief in their ability to solve classroom problems. Teachers who believe that their efforts cannot bring about meaningful change, who have lost hope that anything new will make a difference in their effectiveness or satisfaction, are unlikely to be affected by even the best staff development programs (Sparks, 1983). Teachers with a strong sense of competence and belief in their ability to influence the classroom environment are the most willing to experiment and the most likely to benefit from staff development (Joyce and Showers, 1987). Thus, principals who seek to create a climate for effective staff development should encourage experimentation and promote the self-esteem and sense of self-efficacy which seem to function as prerequisites for a willingness to experiment. For the most practical of reasons, the principal as staff developer should heed the advice of John Gardner (1988D), who wrote, "To help people believe in themselves is one of the leader's highest duties" (p. 23).

4

Forging the Link
Between Cause and Commitment

Stating an organization-wide cause is one thing, but the words mean nothing unless people get committed. Nothing engenders resentment more quickly than ordering someone to be committed. Communication is the critical link between cause and the individual's commitment to it.

— Robert Waterman (1987, p. 319)

What you do is so loud I can't hear what you say.

— Robert Waterman (1987, p. 276)

PRINCIPALS who have clarified the vision of what their schools are trying to become, as well as the values that must be in evidence to move their schools in that direction, have the purposefulness and focus necessary for effective staff development. If they have created a climate in which autonomy, collaboration, and experimentation are valued, they have created the conditions in which staff development programs can flourish. However, it remains for principals to communicate, first, the connection between the vision of the school and a staff development initiative and, second, the contribution each individual can make in achieving this initiative.

Communication serves as the link between organizational cause and the individual's commitment to it, and it is the principal's skill in communicating which forges that link over time. People within the school are entitled to know why they are being asked to do certain things and how they relate to the big picture. It is the responsibility of the principal to convey that information honestly and consistently. In order to fulfill that responsibility, principals should meet face-to-face with teachers individually and in small groups to explain the purpose of a staff development program and how each teacher can help to accomplish that purpose. The notion of patiently explaining intended outcomes and individual roles may not sound like an act of great leadership, but Gardner (1986B) listed "explaining" among the most essential tasks of a leader and contended that "every great leader is surely teaching" (p. 19).

But the skill of a principal in communicating extends

far beyond verbal aptitude. It is the actions of principals, not their exhortations, which communicate most forcefully and effectively. Selective attention and modeling tells others what is truly important to a leader. This strategy of communicating through conscious, continuous attention and modeling can result in greater clarity, consensus, and commitment within the organization. Principals can enhance their skills in communicating by examining their activities in the areas listed below.

1. *Planning.* Principals typically have very little difficulty in keeping occupied during their workday. Studies have consistently shown that their day is characterized by frequent short exchanges and constant interruptions (Leithwood, 1990). They can walk into their offices and spend the entire day reacting to the concerns, issues, and problems that others raise. Effective principals, however, establish short-range and long-range plans to accomplish specific goals (Cawelti, 1984). These plans indicate what is important and can be used to communicate priorities. If the long-range plans of principals focus on the specific staff development efforts which are needed for school improvement, if their day-to-day planning allows them to devote sufficient time and attention to staff development efforts, and if they share their plans with staff, principals are using planning as an effective means of communicating the importance of a staff development program.

2. *Modeling.* Several authorities now define leadership in terms of how the leader behaves (Bellon, 1988). Effective principals use their own behavior to exemplify core values, and they reinforce those values consistently in their daily routines (Deal and Peterson, 1990). Principals who hope to convince others to grow professionally must model their own commitment to continual development. If they are quick to identify the need for other individuals and groups to undergo training to update or acquire skills, but slow to recognize that need in

themselves, principals send mixed messages. Sparks (1987) urged principals to demonstrate a commitment to their personal professional development by pursuing training in such areas as consensus and team-building strategies, conducting effective meetings, and group processing. A synthesis of 22 different research studies (Elam, Cramer and Brodinsky, 1986) advised principals to pursue the following developmental activities:

A. Attend seminars and workshops to master the art of clinical supervision.

B. Participate in local, state, and national conferences or conventions.

C. Read at least one new book and twelve articles in professional journals on their craft each year.

D. Study elements and processes of effective instruction.

E. Formulate strategies for initiating and directing staff development activities at the building level.

There are certainly a number of developmental areas which instructional leaders can strive to master. The specific area they choose to pursue is probably less important than the fact that they serve as role models who demonstrate a commitment to acquiring the skills needed to enhance their job performance. A study of "peak performers" from a number of different walks of life found that these high-achieving individuals identified the areas that would significantly impact on their perform- ance and then pursued training in those areas with a passion (Garfield, 1986). Principals who hope to fulfill their own potential and encourage the development of peak performers among their teachers should model a commitment to continual personal development.

3. *Confronting.* If principals wish to communicate the importance of a particular staff development initiative, they must be willing to confront behavior which is detri-

mental to that effort. This call for confrontation may seem in conflict with recommendations for teacher autonomy and collaboration between principals and teachers, but it most definitely is not. Once a school has made a commitment to a particular staff development program, the boundaries of acceptable behavior have been established. It is the job of the principal to protect those boundaries and ensure the success of the program. Principals may emphasize the importance of a program in the most eloquent of terms, but an unwillingness to confront behavior which is clearly contrary to the goals of a staff development initiative calls the credibility of both the principal and the program into question.

Simply put, effective principals are willing to face and deal with conflict (Deal and Peterson, 1990). Principals should certainly not assume a confrontational or adversarial posture in their general dealings with teachers, but just as certainly they should not avoid a confrontation with a teacher when one is warranted. Administrators who have been trained in the human relations school of management are often unwilling to risk confrontations because of the damage they may do to their relationships with teachers. Effective principals, however, recognize the insightfulness in the observation of James MacGregor Burns (1978), who wrote: "Leaders must settle for far less than universal affection. They must accept conflict. They must be able and willing to be unloved" (p. 34). No principal who has advised a teacher that his or her present conduct or performance is unacceptable relishes the thought of that angry teacher replaying the conference in the faculty lounge. The fact of the matter is, however, that these narrations by a staff member who has been confronted advise the rest of the staff of the value a principal places upon a program in a clear and unequivocal way.

4. *Monitoring.* One of the most powerful means by

which a leader can convey the importance of something within an organization is simply by paying attention to it (Peters and Austin, 1985). It is this visible attention of the leader which influences others and gets things done (Waterman, 1987). A principal who devotes considerable time and effort to the continual assessment of a particular condition within a school sends the message that the condition is important. Conversely, not monitoring something indicates that the factor is less than essential, regardless of how often its importance is verbalized. Attention communicates forcefully because it represents a visible commitment of one of the scarcest resources available to principals—time.

Once again, a staff development program should represent the means to an end rather than the end itself. For example, if the teachers in a particular school are trained in cooperative learning strategies, there should be a clear connection between those strategies and the goals of the school. The intended outcome of the training might be to increase student achievement, to impact positively upon student attitudes toward school, or to advance a district goal to teach students to work effectively with others. If the principal's monitoring is limited to checking to see if teachers are using cooperative learning strategies with no attention paid to the effects of those strategies, he or she sends the implicit message that the use of the strategy is the end itself.

One means of visibly paying attention to something is through measurement. Faculty members should be involved in setting realistic standards for assessing the effect of a staff development program, and these effects should be measured regularly. The measurements should also incorporate comparisons. Schools can easily become data-rich but information-poor as they amass data from monitoring. Meaningful information is contained in comparison and should be presented as differences—from what is expected, in past performance, between similar schools, etc. To extend the example of a school encouraging the use of cooperative learning strategies, a principal and staff could compare students taught by teachers using the technique to students taught by those not using it on the following bases:

A. Student Achievement
   1. Performance on a nationally standardized test
     • Mean score
     • Median score
     • Range
     • Percentage of students below national average
     • Percentage of students in each national quartile
   2. Performance on a locally developed criterion-referenced test
     • Mean score
     • Median score
     • Range
     • Percentage failing to achieve mastery for total test
     • Percentage failing to achieve mastery for each subtest

B. Student Attitudes
   1. Completion of survey of classroom climate
   2. Completion of survey of attitudes toward school
   3. Attendance rates
   4. Frequency and severity of discipline referrals

C. Ability to Work with Others
   1. Present students with complex problems or task requiring cooperation and have observers provide anecdotal accounts of student behavior
   2. Review teacher logs or diaries of student behavior in group work over a period of time

If teachers are resistant to teacher-to-teacher comparisons, a principal and staff could structure the analyses so that each teacher could compare one of his or her classes using cooperative learning strategies with another that does not. Yet another strategy would have teachers apply the evaluation criteria to students from two different school years, one in which the teacher used cooperative learning and the other in which he or she did not. The specific monitoring strategy is less important than the fact that principals develop the means to assess the impact of a staff development program in terms of student outcomes. If principals hope to make staff development a priority, they must develop such monitoring systems and share their evaluation strategies with the staff.

5. *Celebrating*. When teachers have expended effort over a considerable period of time in the pursuit of a staff development program, principals must make certain that recognition is forthcoming. Important initiatives lose their impact and are unable to survive in the absense of celebration. Public attention and recognition serve not only as reinforcement for those who receive it, but as a reminder to others that their contributions will be noticed and celebrated as well.

People tend to judge their own performance by comparing it with others'. A principal who exhorts teachers to be "excellent" fails to give meaningful direction due to the nebulousness of the term. Celebrating the efforts and achievements of individual teachers provides others on the staff with a model and a meaningful yardstick by which they can measure their own performance.

If celebrations are to be effective in communicating the importance of a program and motivating a staff to sustain their efforts in its pursuit, all teachers must feel that they have the opportunity to be recognized for their contributions to a successful program. They must all feel that they can be regarded as winners. Extravagant awards are more likely to result in jealousy than mutual celebration. Principals have used certificates, small plaques, pins, T-shirts, and even the presentation of a rose to honor teachers who have made a significant contribution to a staff development initiative. An achievement need not be monumental to warrant celebration, nor should principals be concerned that they are offering too much recognition, provided that it is given with sincerity. Principals should seek out the small successes in staff development programs and share them with their teachers in order to fuel the continued efforts necessary to sustain the program.

ATTENTION TO THE INSTITUTIONALIZATION OF CHANGE

Administration attention helps to emphasize that a particular innovation is a priority and to persuade teachers to initiate the change process (Miles, 1983). However, the importance of the attention of the principal in a school-improvement effort is not limited to the early stages of the program. Initial success in a school-improvement initiative does not insure its continued impact upon a school. Funding cuts, declining enrollment, and changing personnel all serve as threats to the long-term stability of staff development programs aimed at school improvement. If the benefits of a staff development program are to become truly institutionalized, principals must be attentive to initiating changes in organizational structure, rules, and procedures which stabilize and protect the program.

The nature of the change may depend upon the nature of the particular staff development program. Job descriptions can be rewritten to include the essentials of the innovation with a corresponding alteration in evaluation procedures. A permanent position for program coordinator can be established. Orientation programs can be developed for new and reassigned staff members. Line items can be established in the school budget. Curriculum guidelines can be revised to include the program. The objective is simply to establish the program as part of the routine of the school.

The research on successful school improvement has described this attention to institutionalization as critical to successful school change (Loucks and Zacchei, 1983). Principals cannot afford to leave the institutionalization of a staff development program to chance. At the same time they are working to assist teachers in applying the content of the program in classrooms, they must be attentive to the organizational initiatives which can help to secure the future of that program and its objectives (Cox, 1983). This attention to the institutionalization of the goals of a staff development program is one of the most powerful methods of communicating the importance of that program to a staff.

CHECKING FOR CLARITY

Principals can assess the clarity of their communication by considering a series of questions regarding their activities for the previous thirty days (Bellon, 1988). Appropriate questions for principals who hope to serve as staff developers would include the following:

1. Have I developed and/or addressed long-range plans which focus on the staff development efforts needed for school improvement?

2. Has my day-to-day planning provided me with sufficient time to address staff development objectives?

3. Have I shared the objectives of the staff development plan with faculty and discussed how each of them can contribute to obtaining the objective?

4. Do I communicate positive attitudes and my con-

viction that we have the ability to bring about significant school improvement?

5. Do I have a plan for my own professional growth and self-renewal?

6. Do I have procedures in place to monitor the progress and effects of the staff development program?

7. Do I share the results of monitoring procedures with the staff?

8. Do I encourage collaboration among staff members through creation of small teams and peer observation programs?

9. Has my own relationship with staff reflected professional collaboration rather than authoritarian demands?

10. Have I encouraged teachers to exercise their autonomy and to experiment?

11. Have I confronted behavior which is contrary to school values or the objectives of the staff development program?

12. Have I publicly recognized the hard work of individual staff members and celebrated progress in our staff development program?

13. Have I initiated steps to institutionalize the program and its objectives?

5

Effective
Staff Development Practices

To be effective, to change the professional lives of educators, inservice education simply cannot be something that is *done* to passive participants. Or else there is no real education taking place at all. In that case "inservice" is truly a verb. But it shouldn't be.

— Robert Cole (1982, p. 370)

Stronger training, combined with involvement-oriented governance and the positive effects of organizational leadership, can lay the basis for some very effective staff development.

— Beverly Showers, Bruce Joyce and
Barrie Bennett (1987, p. 87)

UNTIL RECENT YEARS, the issue of staff development in American education was very much like the weather — everyone complained about it but no one seemed to know how to improve it. As recently as 1982, one of the leading educational journals railed against the inservice training of teachers as "one of the most frustrating aspects of the entire education enterprise," a feckless activity with a conceptual basis that was "wrong-headed, doomed to failure," and certain to "breed cynicism and apathy" (Cole, 1982, p. 370).

Fortunately, the attention paid to staff development in the past decade has helped to clarify what steps can be taken to provide effective training for educators. The research has demonstrated how training programs can be purposefully designed, sequenced, and presented to resolve the concerns of teachers and increase the likelihood of their active engagement in the training. There is an increased appreciation of the significant role that adequate time and sufficient support play in the successful implementation of a staff development program. Finally, there is a greater awareness of the importance of organizational leadership to the entire improvement process.

In short, today the topic of staff development can be approached with a much greater level of confidence in our ability to identify "what works." The lessons we have learned from the research provide a useful framework for effective staff development programs. This chapter will attempt to summarize those lessons.

EFFECTIVE PROGRAMS ARE PURPOSEFUL

A nationwide study of schooling practices (Goodlad, 1983) concluded that the staff development efforts of most school districts can be characterized as fragmented and unfocused, lacking clear priorities, common commitment, or school-wide emphasis. In contrast, effective staff development programs are firmly rooted in the goals and vision of a district (Elam, Cramer and Brading, 1986). These programs are designed to meet identified priorities and to promote the values necessary to advance the school (Lieberman and Miller, 1981). Furthermore, a conscious effort is made to clarify the objectives of the training program and to ensure that all staff members are aware of the relationship between those objectives and the overall improvement goals of the school (Loucks-Horsley and Hergert, 1985).

EFFECTIVE PROGRAMS ARE DESIGNED TO PROMOTE AND INFLUENCE TEACHERS' THINKING ABOUT TEACHING

"Successful teachers are thoughtful teachers," wrote Carl Glickman (1986, p. 99), and thus he argued that helping teachers develop their ability to think about what they do should represent the aim of all staff development programs. Research supports the notion that the essential skills which teachers must develop to be more effective in the classroom are cognitive in nature. As one summary of the research concluded:

Behaviors of teachers are directed by thoughts about what to do, when to do it and why. Thus, the purpose of providing training is not, simply, to generate visible teaching moves that bring the practice to bear in the instructional setting, but to generate the cognitions that enable the practice to be selected and used appropriately and integratively (Showers, Joyce and Bennett, 1987, p. 85).

The ultimate goal of training programs is not to create individuals who unthinkingly follow a cookbook approach to teaching, but to develop thoughtful professionals who have the ability to assess and revise their own actions in order to improve the likelihood of success for their students. Glickman (1986) described this ability to make assessments of and revisions to an immediate concrete experience as "abstract thought." Challenging teachers to discuss the whys and hows of what they do is the most effective means of developing their ability to think abstractly. Staff development programs should be designed to ensure that this discussion takes place on an ongoing basis.

EFFECTIVE PROGRAMS ARE RESEARCH-BASED
BOTH IN CONTENT AND PROCESS

Effective staff development programs make use of available knowledge bases. Exemplary practices that have been proven successful should be the very cornerstone of a school improvement effort. If teachers are asked to devote their time and energy to a new program or practice, there should be compelling evidence that the innovation actually makes a difference in teacher effectiveness and the success of students.

The research also presents a clear picture of the most appropriate design for a training program. Virtually all teachers are able to reach levels of understanding that enable them to practice their new skill in their classrooms if their training includes the following steps:

1. Presentation of theory behind the innovation
2. Demonstration
3. Initial practice in the training session
4. Prompt feedback about their efforts

(Showers, Joyce and Bennett, 1987)

However, one of the most consistent and emphatic messages of the research is that teachers need sustained practice in the classroom and frequent coaching in order to gain mastery of a new skill or strategy (Fielding and Schalock, 1985; Loucks-Horsley and Hergert, 1985; Showers, Joyce and Bennett, 1987; Sparks, 1983). Teachers must utilize a new skill twenty to thirty times before they have sufficient mastery to incorporate it within their teaching repertoire, utilize it comfortably, and adapt it to the needs of their students (Showers, Joyce and Bennett, 1987). Coaching—the provision of ongoing feedback and support—promotes this sustained practice. The bad news is that, without the benefit of coaching from either supervisors or peers, teachers are unlikely to sustain practice until they have gained mastery of a new skill regardless of their initial enthusiasm or the skill of the trainer. The good news, however, is that, with coaching, "nearly all teachers [are able] to sustain practice and gain executive control over a large range of curricular and instructional practices" (Showers, Joyce and Bennett, 1987, p. 86). Principals must recognize that providing teachers with ongoing feedback and support *after* initial training is critical to the success of an innovation.

One of the major differences between effective principals and others is that they manage their time in a way that enables them to devote considerable attention to instruction (Cawelti, 1984). But even the best principals will be hard pressed to devote the time and attention that coaching requires for more than a few teachers at a time. Peer coaching offers a promising solution to this problem. As one study (Fielding and Schalock, 1985) concluded:

It is clear that coaching is a potentially powerful approach to increasing teacher effectiveness. . . . It is also clear that teachers can be trained to serve as supportive and effective peer coaches (p. 31).

As in so many other areas, the principal serves as the key to a successful peer coaching program (Joyce, 1987). Peer coaching requires both attention to training and the provision of a structure which enables teachers to engage in the peer coaching process, and principals are in a position to see to it that these essential ingredients are in place. Peer coaching is *not* simply encouraging teachers to visit each other's classrooms. Teachers must be trained in methods of data collection, analysis of teacher behaviors, and elements of effective conferencing if they are to function as effective peer coaches. Principals can demonstrate that they value peer coaching if they ensure that such training is forthcoming.

Furthermore, provisions must be made to enable teachers to work together in pairs or in small teams, to observe each other as they practice new skills, and to meet periodically to discuss their analyses and share their impressions. Principals can free teachers from their other duties and thereby provide them with the time that peer coaching requires by such strategies as:

1. Substituting for teachers themselves
2. Recruiting volunteer aides to assume responsibility for some of the non-teaching duties of the staff
3. Encouraging independent study and research for students in the school library
4. Organizing team teaching
5. Seeking out student teachers
6. Using audio- or videotapes to record and present lessons
7. Hiring substitute teachers

(Joyce and Showers, 1987)

As one study (Showers, Joyce and Bennett, 1987) concluded, "Until alternatives are developed, coaching or its equivalent appears to be essential if the investment in [teacher] training is not to be lost" (p. 57). Principals who embrace their role as staff developers should do everything possible to ensure that this critical component of a training program is in place in their schools.

EFFECTIVE PROGRAMS HAVE REALISTIC TIMEFRAMES

Two of the most common pitfalls of staff development programs involve the issue of time — the time devoted to training and the time needed to bring the improvement project to closure. The research is quite clear that little growth occurs as a result of a single training session. Multiple-day workshops without follow-up sessions are almost equally ineffective. The best schedule for training offers several workshops of two to six hours separated by two or three weeks (Sparks, 1987). When training is presented at such intervals, teachers can avoid information overload, attempt new techniques, and share their findings and frustrations at the next training session.

An even more critical issue in the success of a staff development program is recognition of the fact that effective programs encompass long periods of time. In her study of innovative organizations, Rosabeth Moss Kanter (1983) found that one of the most common mistakes of organizations that were unsuccessful in their attempts at innovation was failure to see the project through to its conclusion. This same failure is typical of school improvement efforts (McGreal, 1988). Teachers and administrators have routinely been denied the opportunity to see a new program or initiative through to maturity. No sooner do schools implement an improvement effort than new issues arise or different priorities are set. As a result, an entire generation of educators has been conditioned to respond to new initiatives with a "this-too-shall-pass" attitude.

The tendency of schools to expect immediate results

from a staff development program has been described as "patently absurd," and the practice of premature evaluations has been likened to "pulling up the flowers every week to see how they are doing" (Loucks-Horsley and Hergert, 1985, p. 50). One study concluded that successful implementation of innovation requires a minimum of two to three years. McGreal (1988) argued that an improvement project requires a three- to five-year commitment in order to have a chance to succeed. While researchers may suggest different timetables for staff development programs, their central message is clear and consistent — those who initiate a staff development program must be prepared both to make a long-term commitment and to take the long view in assessing results.

EFFECTIVE STAFF DEVELOPMENT PROGRAMS ARE EVALUATED AT SEVERAL DIFFERENT LEVELS

Evaluation of staff development programs is often limited to an assessment of the feelings of the participants regarding the training they have received. While this assessment of the training process is useful, it is not a reliable or powerful predictor of actual implementation (Little, 1982, p. 28). Evaluation efforts must be extended to the intended results as well. Principals must concern themselves - both with gathering evidence that what teachers learn in their training gets applied in classrooms and with assessing the effects of the application upon students and teachers. Since principal preparation programs typically fail to provide principals with strategies for assessing the effects of different instructional initiatives, this represents an area in which principals are likely to need additional training if they are to fulfill their responsibilities as staff developers.

The Xerox Corporation evaluates the impact of its training programs by probing for answers at four different levels. The Xerox model can be easily applied to schools. The levels of questions and strategies for answering each level are presented below:

Question	*Method of Data Collection*
1. Did participants enjoy the training?	Questionnaire
2. Did participants learn skills?	Create a task situation for participants to complete and have them evaluate their performance.
3. Did participants use their new skills on the job?	Observers determine whether new skills are being applied in the work place.
4. Did the program affect the bottom line?	Collection of observable, tangible, verifiable facts that show specific profit or performance results.

(Elam, Cramer and Brodinsky, 1986)

The following list presents strategies that might be used to collect rich and relevant data on the impact of a training program:

1. Classroom observations
2. Student performance on criterion-referenced and norm-referenced tests
3. Questionnaires and interviews
4. Official records (for example, attendance, grade distribution, disciplinary referrals, etc.)
5. Teacher logs
6. Classroom artifacts (for example, lesson plans, instructional materials, unit tests, etc.)

EFFECTIVE PROGRAMS GENERATE
TEACHER COMMITMENT TO THE TRAINING

Since the ultimate success of a staff development initiative depends upon the willingness of teachers to commit to that initiative, the task of generating a sense of support and ownership among teachers must be a primary concern of the principal. Conventional wisdom stressed the importance of developing an "up-front" commitment on the part of teachers, and advised that they should be given the opportunity to select, organize, and direct their training in order to promote this initial commitment. This approach continues to have its supporters. As one summary of research (Sparks, 1983) advised:

Several studies of organizational factors and change have concluded that the levels of trust and commitment were higher in programs where participants were involved in project decisions. Collaborative strategies for goal setting, planning and implementation can be valuable tools for developing commitment to professional development activities (p. 15).

An increasing number of studies, however, have found little or no correlation between successful staff development programs and early teacher involvement in the decisions regarding those programs (Crandall, 1987; Fielding and Schalock, 1985; Joyce and Showers, 1987; Loucks-Horsley and Hergert, 1983; Miles, 1983). While not disputing the significance of teacher commitment to the eventual success of a training program, these studies concluded that this commitment can come *after* teachers are engaged in using a new practice, provided that the practice (1) is "user-friendly," that is, easily applied in the classroom, and (2) proves to make a difference in student learning (Sparks and Loucks-Horsley, 1989). As one study (Loucks-Horsley and Hergert, 1983) insisted:

"Thinking you can create ownership at the beginning of a project is ridiculous. Like trust, ownership and commitment build and develop over time through the actual work of improving a school" (p. ix). Another (Showers, Joyce and Bennett, 1987) argued that, without extensive training in a program, teachers lacked sufficient experience or knowledge to make a valid decision about committing to it. Yet another study (Miles, 1983) found that the schools most likely to be successful in institutionalizing a school improvement effort were those in which the process had been mandated and there was considerable stability of personnel. Programs characterized by administrative decisiveness, accompanied by sufficient assistance to increase teachers' skills, were found to be far more likely to result in sustained school improvement than programs launched with initial teacher enthusiasm. The repeated message of these studies is that requiring teacher participation in high-quality programs is entirely defensible. However, principals who conclude that teachers should be ignored in the planning and execution of staff development programs misinterpret the lessons to be derived from this research. As one study (Showers, Joyce and Bennett, 1987) concluded:

People *should* be involved in the social process that surrounds training and should be dealt with as people whose opinions matter. . . . We believe that teacher involvement [in training decisions] is important and desirable (pp. 82–83).

Principals who seek to empower their teachers will generally include them in planning the programs that are intended to enable teachers to improve their effectiveness. This does not, however, mean that principals should not influence these programs and the ways in which they are presented. Principals can involve teachers in the planning of staff development programs at the same time that they provide administrative direction to this important area of the school if they establish parameters within which all programs must operate. One principal gave clear direction to the teacher committee responsible for the selection and preparation of the school's staff development program by insisting that any proposal had to meet the following criteria in order to be adopted by the school:

1. A direct correlation to district or schoolwide goals
2. A strong basis in research
3. A format which provides ongoing training with repeated practice and feedback
4. Frequent opportunities for teacher dialogue and sharing as part of the process
5. A well-articulated evaluation component

Using these criteria, the committee was able to develop programs which appealed to teacher interests, advanced the goals of the school, and corresponded with research findings on characteristics of effective staff development.

Principals must also recognize that teachers who are left to rely on individual preference may sometimes choose to avoid a beneficial new practice if they lack the knowledge and skills needed to assess its benefits. Since meaningful teacher commitment follows competence rather than precedes it, principals should concern themselves less with generating initial enthusiasm for a program and more with providing the assistance to help teachers develop the competence to become committed.

Principals should expect teachers to have concerns about staff development programs regardless of the level of teacher involvement in selecting and planning the program. A degree of concern and anxiety are inevitable by-products of asking people to consider making a change. The Concerns-Based Adoption Model (CBAM) of staff development (Hardy, Rutherford, Huling-Austin and Hall, 1987) has attempted to identify the stages of concern that teachers are likely to experience as they learn about, prepare for, and use a new practice. The stages of concern typically flow from a focus upon self, to managerial issues associated with the task, to the impact of the program. In the early stages, teachers seek information on the innovation — how it is similar to and different from what they are already doing, the nature and extent of the training they are to receive, how they will benefit from that training, etc. As final preparations are made for the teachers to begin utilizing the innovation, task concerns dealing with time become more intense. In the third phase of concerns, teachers address the effects of the innovation upon their students and consider what can be done to improve the effectiveness of the program. If principals make an effort to identify and address these concerns as they emerge, they heighten the potential for the ultimate success of the program. Hord, Rutherford, Austin and Hall (1987) offered the following suggestions for interventions at the various levels of concern:

Stage 0: Awareness Concerns
("What is the innovation?")
- If possible, involve teachers in discussions and decisions about the innovation and its implementation.
- Share enough information to arouse interest, but not so much that it overwhelms.
- Acknowledge that a lack of awareness is expected and reasonable, and that no questions about the innovation are foolish.
- Encourage unaware persons to talk with colleagues who know about the innovation.
- Take steps to minimize gossip and inaccurate sharing of information about the innovation.

Stage 1: Informational Concerns
("I need to know more about the innovation.")

- Provide clear and accurate information about the innovation.
- Use a variety of ways to share information—verbally, in writing, and through any available media. Communicate with individuals and with small and large groups.
- Have persons who have used the innovation in other settings visit with your teachers. Visits to user schools could also be arranged.
- Help teachers see how the innovation relates to their current practices, both in regard to similarities and differences.
- Be enthusiastic and enhance the visibility of others who are excited.

Stage 2: Personal Concerns
("How will the innovation affect me?")

- Legitimize the existence and expression of personal concerns. Knowing that these concerns are common and that others have them can be comforting.
- Use personal notes and conversations to provide encouragement and reinforce personal adequacy.
- Connect these teachers with others whose personal concerns have diminished and who will be supportive.
- Show how the innovation can be implemented sequentially rather than in one big leap. It is important to establish expectations that are attainable.
- Do not push innovation use, but encourage and support it while maintaining expectations.

Stage 3: Management Concerns
("How will I find time to do this?")

- Clarify the steps and components of the innovation.
- Provide answers that address the small, specific

"how-to" issues that are so often the cause of management concerns.

- Demonstrate exact and practical solutions to the logistical problems that contribute to these concerns.
- Help teachers sequence specific activities and set timelines for their accomplishments.
- Attend to the immediate demands of the innovation, not what will be or could be in the future.

Stage 4: Consequence Concerns
("How is my use of the innovation affecting kids?")

- Provide these individuals with opportunities to visit other settings in which the innovation is in use and to attend conferences on the topic.
- Provide them with positive feedback and needed support.
- Find opportunities for these staff members to share their skills with others.
- Share information pertaining to the innovation with them.

Stage 5: Collaboration
("I would like to discuss my findings and ideas with others.")

- Provide these individuals with opportunities to develop those skills necessary for working collaboratively.
- Bring together these persons, both within and outside the school, who are interested in collaboration.
- Help the collaborators establish reasonable expectations and guidelines for the collaborative effort.
- Use them to provide technical assistance to others who need assistance.
- Encourage the collaborators, but do not attempt to force collaboration on those who are not interested.

Stage 6: Refocusing Concerns
("I have an idea for improving upon the innovation.")

- Respect and encourage the interest that these persons have for finding a better way.
- Help channel their ideas and energies in ways that will be productive rather than counterproductive.
- Encourage them to act on their concerns for program improvement.
- Help them access the resources they may need to refine their ideas and put them into practice.
- Be aware of and willing to accept the fact that these staff members may replace or significantly modify the existing innovations.

One of the most effective means of resolving teacher concerns is simply to provide a structure which promotes dialogue among teachers (Lieberman and Miller, 1981; Sparks, 1987). There is growing evidence that creating small, supportive groups in which teachers are encouraged to discuss their questions, concerns, and ideas about a new program enhances the eventual adoption of the program. Groups should be kept to eight or fewer participants in order to encourage discussion and should have the benefit of a facilitator to help keep the group focused on solutions. Having the opportunity to discuss problems they may be encountering in the attempt to implement new ideas helps to reduce the isolation that teachers often feel in initiating a new program. Furthermore, the small-group format provides a forum for the sharing of successes and testimonials needed to fuel the improvement effort. In short, giving teachers the opportunity to discuss the application of the ideas presented in an improvement program is a critically significant aspect of staff development and teacher growth.

EFFECTIVE STAFF DEVELOPMENT PROGRAMS
HAVE STRONG ADMINISTRATIVE SUPPORT

Once again, the importance of strong administrative support, particularly that of the principal, is another of the characteristics of the effective staff development programs documented by research. Administrative indifference results in the inevitable death of training programs (Miles, 1983). Principals who hope to ensure the success of school improvement efforts must concentrate upon clarifying the goals of the program and their relationship to school goals, protecting teachers from competing demands on their time, providing ready access to technical and institutional support, communicating the importance of the program by giving it the attention warranted by a high priority, and providing a realistic timeframe for improvement.

6

Linking Staff Development with Teacher Supervision

Staff development promotes new learning, while supervision increases the teacher's ability to use what has already been learned.

— Fred Wood and Sharon Lease (1987, p. 53)

Clearly it is possible to build processes for increasing the level of talk about teaching through integration of staff development and teacher evaluation.

—Thomas McGreal (1988, p. 4)

THE CONCEPT of staff development is typically linked with groups — an entire faculty is exposed to strategies for promoting critical thinking, the members of a mathematics department develop techniques to get students more actively engaged in the lesson, a group of elementary school teachers agree to receive training in a new program of classroom management. However, attention to staff development should not be limited to group activities. Principals who hope to function as staff developers will recognize that the best opportunities for professional growth often occur in small groups or individual settings. While being attentive to providing quality group programs when appropriate, they must also take advantage of the opportunity to promote professional growth one teacher at a time.

CLINICAL SUPERVISION

Staff development and teacher observation/assessment have been regarded as separate processes in most schools. Teachers typically associate observation/assessment models with teacher evaluation and often do not perceive the process as helpful (Wise and Darling-Hammond, 1985). But if principals utilize the assumptions and processes of clinical supervision as the basis of their procedures for observation/assessment, it is possible that those procedures can both complement and supplement a staff development program. It has been suggested earlier in this book that effective staff development programs result in teachers thinking and talking about teaching.

Clinical supervision can provide a systematic process in which this reflection and discussion takes place.

Whereas staff development programs can enable teachers to acquire new understanding and instructional skills that will increase their effectiveness in the classroom, clinical supervision can help teachers become more proficient as they attempt to apply and refine those skills. Furthermore, analysis of the data collected during supervisory cycles provides principals with the information they need to plan staff development programs that match the real needs of teachers. In short, the process of staff development and clinical supervision can and should go hand-in-hand. Clinical supervision serves as a means of integrating staff development and observation/assessment in a way that advances the intended purpose of both—increasing the effectiveness of the school and its instructional staff.

The key to the integration of staff development and clinical supervision are the assumptions and processes which guide principals in their approach to supervision. If they regard observation/assessment as a process for the rating or ranking of subordinates or as a perfunctory task to be accomplished as painlessly as possible, the collaborative discussion about teaching essential to staff development is unlikely to take place. Principals who hope to function as staff developers should utilize the assumptions and processes of clinical supervision espoused by Morris Cogan and others in order to create the conditions in which the supervisory process promotes professional growth. Clinical supervision has been called "the most potent instrument for teacher improvement" (Elam, p. 33). Some of its basic principles are as follows:

1. The primary goal of clinical supervision is to improve instruction by observing, analyzing, and ulti-

mately changing the behavior that takes place in the classroom.

2. Clinical supervision requires a face-to-face relationship between the principal and the teacher. As Robert Goldhammer (1969) observed, "clinical supervision is meant to imply supervision up close . . . in every case the notion of face-to-face contact will be fundamental" (p. 54).

3. A major purpose of this approach to supervision is to help the teacher see, as objectively as possible, what is actually taking place in the classroom. The process is designed to deal with performance, not personality; behavior, not persons.

4. Clinical supervision works best when the relationship between the principal and teacher is characterized by mutual trust and collegiality.

5. Clinical supervision encourages the professional and personal autonomy of the teacher.

Clinical supervision aims to help teachers become more proficient as they refine their teaching skills and strategies. It utilizes a systematic procedure which includes a preconference, direct observation in the classroom, feedback from the observer, and joint planning of strategies for the teacher to improve current practice. The clinical supervision model developed by Jerry Bellon (1982) is particularly well suited for establishing a link between clinical supervision and staff development. In the pre-observation conference, the principal poses a series of questions which not only allow the observer to gain an understanding of the teacher's intent for the lesson, but also encourages the teacher to mentally rehearse the lesson. These questions (Bellon, 1982) include:

1. What is the relationship of the current unit of study to the course or program goals?

2. What are the students like? Are there students with special needs or characteristics?

3. What will students be able to do as a result of the lesson?

4. What will students be doing during the lesson?

5. What process was used to determine the level of student readiness for the lesson?

6. What process will be used to determine whether or not students have achieved the objectives?

7. What resources and teaching techniques will be utilized?

The teacher is encouraged to do most of the talking during the pre-observation conference, and the principal avoids making value judgments or critiquing answers.

The task of the principal during the observation is to gather objective data that will be useful in the assessment of the effectiveness of the lesson. The observation may be focused on the students or on the teacher, and can be global in nature or narrowly focused (Sparks and Loucks-Horsley, 1989). Once again, the principal avoids recording value judgments during the observation. The principal records what is actually happening in the classroom, rather than his or her feelings about what is happening. For example, at a given point in the lesson the principal might write in his or her observation log, "Three students have heads on desk, two girls talking, boy in last seat of first row working on homework from another class." It would not be appropriate, however, to record that "students seem inattentive."

In the post-observation conference, the teacher and principal discuss the data collected during the observation. In the first stage of the conference, the principal and teacher reconstruct what occurred in the classroom using the data collected and their recollections. Once they have agreed that their reconstruction represents an accurate reflection of what took place, the principal asks the teacher to identify patterns, trends, or recurring teacher or student behaviors in the lesson. The teacher is then asked to assess whether each pattern helped to achieve the intended objective, interfered with the achievement of the objective, or had no bearing on student achievement of the objective. The principal responds to these assessments on the part of the teacher and offers his or her own assessment. Finally, the principal and teacher plan for future instruction, discussing strategies to eliminate negative patterns and identifying areas of focus for the next observation.

The entire cycle — pre-observation conference, observation, and post-observation conference — is repeated three or four times during the year in order to provide the teacher with feedback on the new instructional strategies being practiced. The process is collegial in nature. The goal is not to rate teachers, but to help them develop an analytical approach to teaching that will enable them to monitor and assess their effectiveness even when they are not being observed.

Sparks (1987) has said that "the goal of staff development is growth in the teacher's ability to use knowledge and experience to make enlightened decisions regarding teaching and learning" (p. 23). The same can be said of clinical supervision. It is intended to help teachers reduce their need to rely upon others to assess their effectiveness, and research indicates that its use can positively influence teacher behaviors (Sparks and Loucks-Horsley, 1989). Thus, it represents a potentially powerful form of staff development for principals who develop the skills to use it. Principals who lack training in this critical area should make the acquisition of that training one of their first personal professional development goals.

MATCHING SUPERVISORY STRATEGIES TO
LEVELS OF TEACHER DEVELOPMENT

No single format provides the only structure through which the professional development of teachers can be pursued. There is considerable evidence that staff development is most effective when it takes into account the different needs and levels of readiness of individual teachers (Glickman and Gordon, 1988). Teachers have varying degrees of skill in analyzing instructional problems, developing problem-solving strategies and matching those strategies to specific situations. Teachers with little ability in these areas typically require more specific, concrete direction in terms of problem identification and solution. Teachers with moderate ability benefit from a more collaborative approach to their professional development, one in which the teacher and principal exchange perceptions about problems, assign priorities to them, and jointly generate possible actions to solve them. Gentle negotiation and give-and-take are the norm at this level of development. Finally, teachers who are skilled in identifying problems, visualizing various strategies, anticipating consequences, and selecting the most appropriate response can flourish with a non-directive approach to their professional development — an approach in which the principal simply serves as a colleague who poses questions to help the teacher clarify goals and provides the encouragement and resources to pursue them.

The ultimate goal of staff development is to enable all teachers to reach the degree of professionalism represented by reflective, self-directed teachers. However, principals should recognize that teachers at different levels of professional development may require different supervisory responses to facilitate their professional growth (Glickman and Gordon, 1987).

7

Alternative Approaches to Staff Development

Support, encouragement, advice, choices, coaching, resources, and team work are the substantive tools of staff development.
— Kenneth Dunn (1988, p. 1)

Cooperative staff development is characterized by the joining together of two or more teachers or administrators to solve a perceived problem.
— Georgia Sparks (1987, p. 21)

JUST as no single supervisory posture is well suited to promoting the professional growth of teachers, no single format provides the optimum structure for staff development activities. Research supports the notion that teachers can grow through various processes (Sparks and Loucks-Horsley, 1989). The following discussion highlights just some of the possible formats for meaningful staff development.

STRUCTURED PROFESSIONAL DIALOGUE

In this strategy, the principal arranges to bring small groups of teachers together on a regular basis for focused discussions of a current development in education and how it applies to their teaching. Some topics might be related to a given subject area, such as using a literature-based reading program, teaching values through social studies, or weighing the merits of the new standards for teaching mathematics proposed by the National Council of Teachers of Mathematics. Others might cut across disciplines: assessing the impact of ability-grouping on student learning, teaching writing across the curriculum, or promoting critical thinking. The most suitable topics are those which have direct impact on the classroom, some difference of professional opinion regarding the issue, and sufficient available background material and resources (Glatthorn, 1987). Responsibility for leading the discussion may reside with the principal, a teacher recognized as proficient in the topic, or members of the group on a rotating basis.

Each discussion session follows a three-step format. In the first, the group considers a summary of the views of experts and research findings. Members then analyze, not dispute, that information. To what extent do experts agree? What issues divide them? Do research findings conflict? In the second step, discussion focuses on the sharing of personal experience and knowledge. In what way does the experience of each teacher support or refute the position of experts or findings of research? Participants are encouraged to neither mindlessly accept the external information nor foolishly reject it. The final step focuses on significance of the discussion for the participants' classrooms. Teachers attempt to build connections between the professional dialogue and their future practices. Subsequent discussions focus on the success of their efforts, the effectiveness of various strategies, modifications they have found helpful, etc. Structured professional dialogue provides an excellent means of engaging teachers in reflection upon and discussion about teaching and learning (Glatthorn, 1987).

ACTION RESEARCH

While action research can be done by teachers working alone, it often brings together two or more teachers who identify a problem and develop a workable solution. After the group identifies and defines the problem it intends to address, it develops an action plan and timeline for the project. Members develop strategies for gathering information about the problem — from reviewing existing research to gathering original classroom or school-wide data. Once this information has been considered, changes are made and new data are gathered and analyzed to determine the effects of the intervention (Sparks and Loucks-Horsley, 1989). Teachers can be called upon to report their findings and share their insight with the rest of the faculty. Action research can facilitate reflection about teaching, promote collegial interaction, foster experimentation, give teachers an opportunity to assume new roles, and close the gap between research and practice (Glatthorn, 1987).

CURRICULUM DEVELOPMENT

Providing teachers with the opportunity to work together to design a curriculum and analyze its impact upon student outcomes is another effective means of promoting collaboration and encouraging reflection upon teaching and learning (Glickman, 1986). One large high school has divided its entire faculty into curriculum teams on the basis of the courses they teach. The process works as follows:

1. All teachers responsible for the same course discuss their beliefs regarding the outcomes each student should achieve as the result of enrollment in that course. As a team, the teachers identify eight to ten outcomes per semester that they agree represent the essential core outcomes of the course.

2. The team selects textbooks and supplementary materials and discusses alternatives for sequencing content and pacing of instruction.

3. The team writes a common course description which explains the general goals of the course, lists the outcomes to be achieved, identifies special projects or assignments, and describes the methods by which grades will be determined. The course description is presented to each student on the first day of the semester.

4. The team writes a criterion-referenced examination with each item referenced to one of the essential outcomes. Members also review released sets of nationally normed exams such as the National Assessment of Educa-

tional Progress and include items which assess student mastery of the essential outcomes. These items provide a national reference point. All students who complete the course are required to take this examination.

5. The team is provided with a computer analysis of the results of the testing. This analysis provides the mean score for the total examination as well as for each sub-test (groups of items covering a single topic). It also provides a summary of student responses on each item of the test. The team reviews the results and gives particular attention to items or subtests in which student performance failed to meet anticipated proficiency levels.

6. The team develops strategies for improving performance. Strategies might include rewriting poor test items, giving greater emphasis to certain topics, revising the sequence or pacing of content, developing supplementary materials, etc. The team provides a written report of its strategies for future instruction to the department chairman and principal.

It has been suggested that action should be preceded by thought and followed by reflection. This curriculum development strategy ensures that sequence and brings teachers together to review such critical questions as what should be taught in our subject area, how might we best teach it, what evidence do we have that students are learning, and what can we do to improve their learning? It is a powerful means of promoting the professional growth of teachers (Sparks and Loucks-Horsley, 1989).

PEER CONSULTATION

This strategy trains small teams of teachers to use clinical supervision to help each other grow professionally. The model developed by Goldsberg (1986) includes nine key characteristics:

1. The process is observation-based: colleagues observe each other teach.

2. The observation is data-based: the observer records full information about the class observed.

3. There is collaborative assessment: each participant tries to identify patterns of teacher and learner behavior.

4. There is a concern for learner outcomes.

5. The collaborative assessment is based upon the learning goals and principles that the teacher has articulated.

6. The process involves a cycle of observation and conferences.

7. The process is confidential.

8. The process has a future orientation: the goal of the consultation is to produce future benefits.

9. There is reciprocal assessment: just as the consultant helps the teacher to improve practice, so should the teacher help the consultant to improve his or her consulting skills.

One principal who found teachers reluctant to try this approach used it as the basis for a mentoring program in which veteran teachers on the staff were linked with teachers new to the district. Teachers who felt uncomfortable about entering into the consultation process with longstanding colleagues were generally quite willing to serve as a mentor, and both mentors and the new teachers consistently reported that the process contributed to the professional growth of both parties.

ARTIFACT COLLECTION

Teaching artifacts include all instructional materials used by teachers to facilitate learning. Many of these materials are developed by the teachers themselves — study guides, question sheets, worksheets, quizzes, tests, dittoed materials, etc. In fact, it has been estimated that students in K–3 classrooms spend over seventy percent of their day with teacher-developed or -selected materials. In Grades 6–12, the time students spend with teacher materials can average between forty and sixty percent of allocated instructional time (McGreal, Broderick and Jones, 1984). The quality of these artifacts and the effectiveness of their day-to-day use can play a significant role in student learning.

Teachers who utilize this process simply collect artifacts for a given teaching unit — lesson plans, all teacher-developed materials, homework assignments, quizzes, exams, etc. At the end of the unit, the teacher and principal attempt to review the materials and assess them according to predetermined criteria. McGreal, Broderick and Jones (1984) suggest the following framework for this assessment:

Content Considerations

The quality of artifacts should be determined by their content or essential meaning. Some considerations related to quality of content are:

1. Validity: Is the artifact accurate and authoritative?

2. Appropriateness: Is the content appropriate to the level of the learner?

3. Relevance: Is the content relevant to the purpose of the lesson?

4. Motivation: Does the artifact stimulate interest to learn more about the subject?

5. Application: Does the artifact serve as a model for applying learning outside the instructional situation?

6. Clarity: Is the content free of words, expressions, and graphics that would limit its comprehension?

7. Conciseness: Is the artifact free of superfluous material? Does it stick to the point?

Design Considerations

Analysis of artifact design should also focus on the content of the lesson or instructional unit. The quality of the artifact is the product of its design characteristics, relevance to instructional objectives, and application to content.

1. Medium selection: Is the most appropriate medium used for meeting each objective and presenting each item of content (films, textbooks, teacher-prepared handout, etc.)?

2. Meaningfulness: Does the artifact clearly support learning objectives? If so, is this apparent to the learner?

3. Appropriateness: Is the design appropriate to the needs and skill levels of the intended learner? Are time constraints considered in the artifact's design?

4. Sequencing: Is the artifact itself sequenced logically? Is it employed at the appropriate point in the presentation?

5. Instructional strategies: Is the artifact format appropriate to the teaching approach? Does its construction incorporate sound learning principals?

6. Engagement: Does the artifact actively engage the learner?

7. Evaluation: Is there a plan for evaluating the artifact's effectiveness when used by the intended learner? Can the success rate for the artifact be easily determined?

Presentation Considerations

Presentation includes the physical and esthetic aspects of an artifact as well as direction for its use.

1. Effective use of time: Is the artifact suitable for the time allotted? Is the learner's time wasted by such things as wordiness or information unrelated to the learning objective?

2. Pace: Is the pace appropriate to the level of the

learners? Does the pace vary inversely with difficulty of content?

3. Aids to understanding: Are directions clearly explained? Are unfamiliar terms defined? Are important concepts emphasized?

4. Visual quality: Do the visuals show all educationally significant details? Are essential details identified through appropriate use of highlighting, color, position, or other devices?

5. Audio quality: Can the audio component be clearly heard?

6. Physical quality: Is the artifact durable and simple? Are size and shape convenient for hands-on use and storage?

This process encourages teachers to regard instructional materials not as an end, but as means to an end. Furthermore, it generates high-level, technical professional talk between teachers and principals (McGreal, Boderick and Jones, 1984).

PREPARATION AND PRESENTATION OF STAFF DEVELOPMENT PROGRAMS

Teachers sometimes learn best from one another and should be encouraged to regard each other as sources of information and assistance (Sparks, 1983). One way to promote that perception is to encourage teachers with an interest or expertise in a particular area of instruction to develop and present a program on the topic to other interested staff. It is quite likely that teachers initially will be reluctant to make presentations before their peers.

An elementary school principal helped to overcome this reluctance by holding the regularly scheduled faculty meetings in a different teacher's room each month. The first twenty minutes of each meeting were set aside to allow the host teachers to talk about something that they were doing in the classrooms. In time, teachers became more comfortable talking about instruction in front of their peers and more willing to assume a leadership role in the presentation of staff development programs (Barth, 1981). Since teachers report that they prefer to receive training from a peer rather than an outside consultant, feel more comfortable exchanging ideas, and regard the information presented by a peer trainer as more practical (Sparks and Loucks-Horsley, 1989), principals should encourage their teachers to prepare and present staff development programs.

SUBMISSION OF ARTICLES FOR PUBLICATION

There is no question that the writing process helps to clarify thinking. Teachers who set out to write an article for professional publication are stimulated to critically examine their beliefs and practices. They must give considerable thought not only to presenting their ideas clearly and coherently, but also to building a rationale to support them. Although the writing process will benefit teachers regardless of whether or not the writing results in publication, many teachers may be unwilling to put forth the effort unless they feel that there is a likelihood of seeing their work in print. A small district helped to resolve that issue by creating its own professional journal, published annually, which featured the writings of its staff. Principals who can stimulate teachers to write about teaching can feel confident that they have succeeded in stimulating teachers to think about teaching.

SELF-ANALYSIS OF VIDEOTAPES

Professional athletes spend hours reviewing video-tapes of their performance, looking for flaws in their technique. Surgeons routinely have operations filmed in order to review their procedures. Teachers, too, can benefit from self-analysis of videotapes of their teaching, particularly if they are provided with a structure with which to conduct the analysis. Since it may take time for both teachers and students to become comfortable with the presence of the video camera in the classroom, it is advisable to videotape a class on two consecutive days at the junior and senior high level, or for two consecutive periods at the elementary school level. Teachers should be advised to concentrate their analysis upon the second half of the tape. After teachers have conducted the self-analysis, they should be encouraged if not required to discuss their conclusions with the principal. If "a picture is worth a thousand words," a videotape can sometimes speak volumes to a teacher.

TEAM TEACHING WITH THE PRINCIPAL

One school that has initiated an interesting variation on the common practice of team teaching encourages teachers to team teach with the principal. The teacher and principal are jointly responsible for planning a two- or three-week unit of instruction, gathering materials, developing strategies for assessment, presenting instruction, working with students, grading papers, etc. They approach the task as peers with the principal recognizing that the teacher has the benefit of personal knowledge of the progress and abilities of each student, and the teacher recognizing that the principal has the benefit of observing many other classrooms from which he or she may have gathered ideas. The practice not only fosters discussion of teaching and learning but gives the principal greater empathy for the actual conditions of teaching and greater credibility with teachers.

A faculty member who is looking for a reason to dispute or ignore the instructional recommendations of a principal has a tendency to fall back on, "Well, it has been years since you were in the classroom, and that won't work now." A principal who team teaches on occasion can diffuse this reaction, particularly if the principal is really good in the classroom and establishes a reputation as an excellent instructor. Finally, by participating in the primary task of the school (teaching and learning), the principal brings recognition to the importance of those tasks (DuFour, 1986).

Since an insecure teacher may regard a proposal to team teach with the principal as an invasion of privacy or threat to security, principals should initiate this process with their most capable, confident teachers in order to demonstrate that their intent is promoting the professional growth that can be gained through team teaching rather than devising a scheme for spying on teachers. Once the program and its intent is well established, less confident teachers can be included.

EMPOWERING TEACHERS

A veteran principal observed that "any initiative emanating from a teacher carries with it a potential for professional growth" (Barth, 1981, p. 145). Principals should be particularly attentive to the important task of identifying and supporting champions—zealous advocates who are willing to become personally committed to the success of an idea. The eventual outcome of an innovation depends more on the advocacy of an eager champion than the passive acquiescence of the many. Teacher compliance with programs and practices which are imposed upon them is likely to last only as long as an administrator is there to monitor and supervise. Changes which emanate from teachers, on the other hand, last until they find a better way. Furthermore, if a teacher initiates a change and demonstrates its effectiveness, it is likely that his or her colleagues will soon follow. If a teacher is willing to advance an idea, the principal should do everything possible to support that individual. The recognition, encouragement, and nurturing of champions is a key task for the principal as staff developer.

CONCLUSION

The Renewing School

All renewal is a blend of continuity and change. . . . We are buffeted by events over which we have no control, and change will occur. The question is, will it be the kind of change that will preserve our deepest values, enhance the vitality of the system, and insure its future?

— John Gardner (1986B, p. 22)

A KEY to the ongoing effectiveness of any organization is its ability to renew itself—to seek and find better ways of fulfilling its mission and responding to change. In some schools, problems may be so obvious that a staff becomes dissatisfied and enthusiastically seeks change. Typically, however, in schools as in most organizations, those within the organization accept things as they are. Innovation is blocked by a thicket of habits, fixed attitudes, settled procedures, and unquestioned assumptions. The conditions found in public education—levels of bureaucracy, the complacency that can accompany tenure, the virtual monopolies within a given geographic area—can accelerate this tendency toward unthinking acceptance of the status quo. The existing way of doing things can rapidly harden into inviolable routines both for individual teachers and an entire school.

The problem can be avoided only if principals recognize that one of their most important responsibilities is to create a school-wide commitment to the constant search for a better way of teaching and learning. As Robert Waterman (1987) wrote, "Without renewal there can be no excellence. We need to introduce fresh energy into the system to stave off the inexorable forces of decay. . . .[Renewal] is a constant challenge, never. . .quite. . . solved. . ." (p. 21).

If principals are to help their schools become renewing organizations, they must recognize several important realities. First, the only true source of renewal in a school is people. It is the efforts of individuals, not programs, policies, or prescriptions that hold the key to school improvement. Second, individuals cannot achieve renewal if they do not believe in the possibility of it. As Joyce and Murphy (1990) observed: "If the culture of a school is permeated with a belief that the causes of student learning lie largely *outside* the school, in the genes and social background of the students, school improvement efforts may appear hopeless and even ridiculous" (p. 248). Principals must help both teachers and students to believe in themselves and their capacity to bring about improved results. Third, this optimism and confidence must be accomplished by the realization that organizational renewal is difficult. Setbacks are bound to occur, and every experiment will not prove successful. Bennis and Nanus (1985), who interviewed over one hundred successful leaders, found that they never used the word "failure" but used such synonyms as "mistake" or "glitch" to describe attempts gone awry. Although they certainly had failures, they viewed them as situations from which they could learn and thus improve the likelihood of their success in their subsequent efforts. Principals must help teachers see temporary failure and frustration not as a reason to doubt themselves but as a reason to strengthen their resolve.

This same call for a balance of optimism and realism is extended to principals as the concluding message of this book. Principals who recognize that school improvement means people improvement and commit themselves to creating the conditions to promote the professional growth of their teachers, can make an enormous difference in their schools. But it will not be easy. In the final analysis, their ultimate success will be a function of their persistence. Hyman Rickover (1985) observed that, "Good ideas and innovations must be driven into existence by courageous patience" (p. 415). May principals who accept their responsibilities as staff developers have the perseverence and "courageous patience" necessary to fulfill that role.

Bibliography

American Association of School Administrators. 1986. *Staff Development: Problems and Solutions.* Arlington, Va.: AASA Press.

Barth, Roland. 1981. "The Principal as Staff Developer." *Journal of Education.* 163 (1) 144–62.

Bellon, Jerry. 1988. "The Dimensions of Leadership." *Vocational Education Journal.* November/December. 29–31.

Bennis, Warren, and Burt Nanus. 1985. *Leaders: The Strategies for Taking Charge.* New York: Harper and Row.

Boyer, Ernest L. 1983. *A Report on Secondary Education in America.* New York: Harper and Row.

————. 1988. "School Reform: Completing the Course." *NASSP Bulletin.* 72 (504) 61–68.

Carnegie Forum on Education and the Economy. 1986. *A Nation Prepared: Teachers for the Twenty-First Century.* Washington, D.C.: Carnegie Foundation.

Cawelti, Gordon. 1984. "Behavior Patterns of Effective Principals." *Educational Leadership.* 41 (5) 3.

Cox, Pat L. 1983. "Complementary Roles in Successful Change." *Educational Leadership.* 41 (3) 10–13.

Crandall, David. 1983. "The Teacher's Role in School Improvement." *Educational Leadership.* 41 (3) 6–9.

Deal, Terrence, and Allan Kennedy. 1982. *Corporate Cultures: The Rites and Rituals of Corporate Life.* Reading, Mass.: Addison–Wesley.

————, and Kent Peterson. 1990. *The Principal's Role in Shaping School Culture.* Washington, D.C.: U.S. Department of Education.

Della-Dora, Delmo. 1987. "Quality Supervision and Organization for Quality Teaching." *Educational Leadership.* 44 (8) 35–38.

Dillon-Peterson, Betty. 1986. "Trusting Teachers to Know What's Good for Them." In *Improving Teaching.* Alexandria, Va.: ASCD Press.

Doggett, Maran. 1987. "Staff Development: Eight Leadership Behaviors for Principals." *NASSP Bulletin*. 71 (497) 1-10.

DuFour, Richard, and Robert Eaker. 1987. *Fulfilling the Promise of Excellence: A Practitioner's Guide to School Improvement.* Westbury, N.Y.: Wilkerson Publishing.

————. 1986. "A Principal Returns to the Classroom." *NASSP Bulletin*. 70 (487) 106-9.

Dunn, Kenneth. 1988. *Staff Development/Inservice.* Reston, Va.: NASSP Press.

Elam, Stanley; Jerome Cramer, and Ben Brodinsky. *Staff Development: Problems and Solutions.* Arlington, Va.: AASA Press.

Fielding, Glen, and H. Del Schalock. 1985. *Promoting the Professional Development of Teachers and Administrators.* Eugene, Ore.: Center for Educational Policy and Management.

Fullan, Michael. 1990. "Staff Development, Innovation and Institutional Development." In *Changing School Culture Through Staff Development.* Alexandria, Va.: ASCD Press.

Gardner, John. 1986A. *The Nature of Leadership.* Washington, D.C.: The Independent Sector.

————. 1986B. *The Tasks of Leadership.* Washington, D.C.: The Independent Sector.

————. 1986C. *The Heart of the Matter: Leader-Constituent Interaction.* Washington, D.C.: The Independent Sector.

————. 1986D. *Leadership and Power.* Washington, D.C.: The Independent Sector.

————. 1987A. *The Moral Aspects of Leadership.* Washington, D.C.: The Independent Sector.

————. 1987B. *Attributes and Context.* Washington, D.C.: The Independent Sector.

————. 1987C. *Leadership Development.* Washington, D.C.: The Independent Sector.

————. 1987D. *Constituents and Followers.* Washington, D.C.: The Independent Sector.

————. 1988A. *The Task of Motivating.* Washington, D.C.: The Independent Sector.

————. 1988B. *Renewing: The Leader's Creative Task.* Washington, D.C.: The Independent Sector.

_____. 1988c. *The Changing Nature of Leadership*. Washington, D.C.: The Independent Sector.

_____. 1988d. *Leadership: An Overview*. Washington, D.C.: The Independent Sector.

_____. 1988e. "Principals and Leadership—An Interview with John Gardner." *NASSP Bulletin*. 72 (509) 70–78.

Garfield, Charles. 1986. *Peak Performers: The New Heroes of American Business*. New York: Avon Books.

Garmston, Robert. 1987. "How Administrators Support Peer Coaching." *Educational Leadership*. 44 (5) 18–26.

Georgiades, William; Ernestina Fuentes, and Karolyn Snyder. 1983. *A Meta-Analysis of Productive School Cultures*. Houston: University of Texas.

Glatthorn, Allan. 1987. "Cooperative Professional Development: Peer Centered Options for Teacher Growth." *Educational Leadership*. 45 (3) 31–35.

Glickman, Carl. 1986. "Developing Teacher Thought." *Journal of Staff Development*. 7 (1) 99–113.

_____, and Stephen Gordon. 1987. "Clarifying Developmental Supervision." *Educational Leadership*. 44 (8) 64–70.

Goldsberry, L. F. 1986. "Colleague Consultation: Another Case of Fools Rush In." Paper presented at the annual meeting of the American Educational Research Association (San Francisco). (In Glatthorn. 1987.)

Goodlad, John. 1984. *A Place Called School*. New York: McGraw-Hill.

Hallinger, Phillip, and Joseph Murphy. 1987. "Assessing and Developing Principal Instructional Leadership." *Educational Leadership*. 45 (1) 54–61.

Hord, Shirley M.; William Rutherford; Leslie Huling-Austin, and Gene Hall. 1987. *Taking Charge of Change*. Alexandria, Va.: ASCD Press.

Huberman, A. Michael. 1983. "School Improvement Strategies That Work." *Educational Leadership*. 41 (3) 23–27.

Johnson, David, and Roger Johnson. 1987. "Research Shows the Benefits of Adult Cooperation." *Educational Leadership*. 45 (3) 27–30.

Joyce, Bruce. 1987. "Conversation with Ron Brandt." *Educational Leadership*. 44 (5) 73–77.

————, and Carlene Murphy. 1990. "Epilogue: The Curious Complexities of Cultural Change." In *Changing School Culture Through Staff Development.* Bruce Joyce, editor. Alexandria, Va.: ASCD Press.

————, and Beverly Showers. 1983. *Power in Staff Development Through Research on Teaching.* Alexandria, Va.: ASCD Press.

————. 1987. "Low-Cost Arrangements for Peer-Coaching." *Journal of Staff Development.* 8 (1) 87–91.

Leithwood, Kenneth. 1990. "The Principal's Role in Teacher Development." In *Changing School Culture Through Staff Development.* Alexandria, Va.: ASCD Press.

Lemley, Raymond. 1987. "Basic Behaviors of Leadership Provide Foundation for Principals." *NASSP Bulletin.* 71 (502) 58–60.

Levine, Daniel, and Lawrence Lezotte. 1990. *Unusually Effective Schools: A Review and Analysis of Research and Practice.* Madison, Wis.: The National Center for Effective Research and Development.

Levine, Sarah. 1985. "Translating Adult Development Research Theory into Staff Development Practice." *Journal of Staff Development.* 6 (1) 121–31.

Lewis, Karen Seashore. 1986. "Reforming Secondary Schools: A Critique and Agenda for Administrators." *Educational Leadership.* 44 (1) 33–36.

Lieberman, Ann, and Lynne Miller. 1981. "Synthesis of Research on Improving Schools." *Educational Leadership.* 38 (7) 583–86.

Little, Judith Warren. 1982. "Making Sure: Contributions and Requirements of Good Evaluation." *Journal of Staff Development.* 3 (1) 25–47.

Loucks, Susan. 1983. "At Last: Some Good News from a Study of School Improvement." *Educational Leadership.* 41 (3) 4–5.

Loucks-Horsley, Susan, and Leslie F. Hergert. 1985. *An Action Guide to School Improvement.* Alexandria, Va.: ASCD Press.

Maeroff, Gene. 1988. "Teacher Empowerment: A Step

Toward Professionalization." *NASSP Bulletin.* 72 (511) 52-60.

McEvoy, Barbara. 1987. "Everyday Acts: How Principals Influence Development of Their Staffs." *Educational Leadership.* 44 (5) 73-77.

McGreal, Thomas. 1988. "Evaluation for Enhancing Instruction: Linking Teacher Evaluation and Staff Development." In Sarah Stanley and James W. Popham. *Teacher Evaluation: Six Prescriptions for Success.* Alexandria, Va.: ASCD Press.

———; Eileen Broderick, and Joyce Jones. 1984. *Educational Leadership.* 41 (7) 20-21.

Miles, Matthew B. 1983. "Unravelling the Mystery of Institutionalization." *Educational Leadership.* 41 (3) 14-22.

Norris, Bill. 1988. "Staff Plunged into Gloom by Power Loss." *Times Educational Supplement.* 3753, 17.

Northwest Regional Educational Laboratory. 1984. *Effective Schooling Practices: A Research Synthesis.* Portland, Ore.: Northwest Regional Educational Laboratory.

Ordovensky, Pat. 1989. "Main Events." *Education Vital Signs.* Washington, D.C.: National School Board Association.

Peters, Thomas, and Robert Waterman. 1982. *In Search of Excellence: Lessons from America's Best-Run Companies.* New York: Harper and Row.

———, and Nancy Austin. 1985. *A Passion for Excellence: The Leadership Difference.* New York: Random House.

———. 1988. "In Search of Excellence—A Talk with Tom Peters." *NASSP Bulletin.* 72 (512) 36-45.

Rickover, Hyman. 1985. In Peters and Austin.

Schlecty, Phillip. 1990. Unpublished address to the Leadership Academy of the Lake County, Illinois Educational Service Center) (Woodstock, Ill.).

Sergiovanni, Thomas. 1984. "Leadership and Excellence in Schooling." *Educational Leadership.* 41 (5) 4-13.

Showers, Beverly; Bruce Joyce, and Barrie Bennett. 1987. "Synthesis of Research on Staff Development: A Framework for Future Study and a State-of-the-Art Analysis." *Educational Leadership.* 45 (3) 77-87.

Smith, Wilma F., and Richard L. Andrews. 1989. *Instructional*

Leadership: How Principals Make a Difference. Alexandria, Va.: ASCD Press.

Sparks, Dennis. 1984. "Staff Development and School Improvement: An Interview with Ernest Boyer." *Journal of Staff Development.* 5 (2) 32–39.

————, and Susan Loucks-Horsley. 1989. "Five Models of Staff Development for Teachers." *Journal of Staff Development.* 10 (4) 40–57.

Sparks, Georgia Mohlman. 1983. "Synthesis of Research on Staff Development for Effective Teaching." *Educational Leadership.* 41 (3) 65–72.

————. 1987. *Promoting the Professional Development of Teachers in Career Ladders.* Oxford, Ohio: National Staff Development Council.

Stallings, Jane. 1986. "Using Time Effectively: A Self-Analytical Approach." In *Improving Teaching.* Alexandria, Va.: ASCD Press.

Thompson, Scott. 1980. Foreword to *Improving School Climate* by Edgar Kelley. Reston, Va.: NASSP Press.

United States Department of Education. 1984. *The Nation Responds: Recent Efforts to Improve Education.* Washington, D.C.: U.S. Government Printing Office.

Vaill, Peter. 1984. In "Leadership and Excellence in Schooling" by Thomas Sergiovanni. *Educational Leadership.* 41 (5) 4–13.

Ventures in Good Schooling. 1985. Monograph developed jointly by the National Education Association (Washington, D.C.) and the National Association of Secondary School Principals (Reston, Va.).

Walker, Terrance, and Judith Vogt. 1987. "The School Administrator as Change Agent: Skills for the Future." *NASSP Bulletin.* 71 (502) 41–48.

Waterman, Robert. 1987. *The Renewal Factor.* New York: Bantam Books.

Wildman, Terry, and Jerry Niles. 1987. "Essentials of Professional Growth." *Educational Leadership.* 44 (5) 4–10.

Wise, Arthur, and Linda Darling-Hammond. 1985. "Teacher Evaluation and Teacher Professionalism." *Educational Leadership.* 42 (4) 28–33.

Wood, Fred, and Sharon Lease. 1987. "An Integrated Approach to Staff Development, Supervision and Teacher Evaluation." *Journal of Staff Development.* 8 (1) 52–55.

_____; Steve Thompson, and Sister Frances Russel. 1981. "Designing Effective Staff Development Programs." In *Staff Development/Organizational Development.* Alexandria, Va.: ASCD Press.

Zumwalt, Karen Kepler. 1986. "Working Together to Improve Teaching." In *Improving Teaching.* Alexandria, Va.: ASCD Press.

ABOUT THE AUTHOR

Dr. Richard DuFour is the Superintendent of Adlai Stevenson High School District 125 in Lincolnshire, Illinois. As the Principal of Stevenson High School from 1983 to 1991, he helped the school become the first in Illinois to receive on two occasions the United States Department of Education's Excellence in Education Award. The school has received commendations from the National Center for Effective Schools and the College Board, and has twice been named as one of the top high schools in America by a national magazine.

Dr. DuFour was the first high school principal in Illinois to be presented the state's Distinguished Educator Award and the only high school principal designated as an "Instructional Leader" by the Illinois Principals Association. He has been presented the Distinguished Alumni Award from Illinois State University, was named as one of the "Top 100" School Administrators in the national *Executive Educator* magazine, and was the nation's first principal to be designated as a fellow of the National Center for Effective Schools due to "outstanding contributions to the effective schools movement." He is the author of three books and numerous professional articles. He has also served as an associate professor in three different universities.

Dr. DuFour has conducted institutes for the National Association of Secondary School Principals, the Association for Supervision and Curriculum Development, the National Staff Development Council, the American Association of School Administrators, and the United States Department of Defense (DODDS), as well as presentation to school districts across the United States and Canada.

ABOUT THE EDITOR

Dennis Sparks is Executive Director of the National Staff Development Council. Prior to this position, he served as an independent educational consultant and as Director of the Northwest Staff Development Center, a state and federally funded teacher center located in Livonia, Michigan. Dr. Sparks has also been a teacher, counselor, co-director of an alternative school, and has taught at several universities. He has conducted workshops from coast to coast on topics such as effective teaching, motivating students, staff development, and teacher stress and burnout. He is executive editor of *The Journal of Staff Development* and has written articles that have appeared in a wide variety of publications, including *Phi Delta Kappan, Educational Leadership, Instructor, Today's Education, The Personnel and Guidance Journal,* and *The Michigan School Board Journal,* among others. Dr. Sparks is co-author of the ASCD videotapes *Effective Teaching for Higher Achievement* and *School Improvement through Staff Development,* and he has participated in numerous radio and television productions.

About *The Principal as Staff Developer* and the National Educational Service

The mission of the National Educational Service is to help create environments in which **all** children and youth will succeed. *The Principal as Staff Developer* is just one of many resources and staff development opporutnities we provide that focus on building a Community Circle of Caring. If you have any questions, comments, articles, manuscripts, or youth art you would like us to consider for publication, please contact us at the address below.

Staff Development Opportunities Include:

Improving Schools through Quality Leadership
Integrating Technology Effectively
Creating Professional Learning Communities
Building Cultural Bridges
Discipline with Dignity
Ensuring Safe Schools
Managing Disruptive Behavior
Reclaiming Youth At Risk
Working with Today's Families

National Educational Service
1252 Loesch Road
Bloomington, IN 47404
(812) 336-7700
(800) 733-6786
FAX (812) 336-7790
e-mail: nes@nes.org
WWW: http://www.nes.org/

NEED MORE COPIES OR ADDITIONAL RESOURCES ON THIS TOPIC?

Need more copies of this book? Want your own copy? Need additional resources on this topic? If so, you can order additional materials by using this form or by calling us at (800) 733-6786 or (812) 336-7700. Or you can order by FAX at (812) 336-7790.

Preview any resource for 30 days without obligation. If you are not completely satisfied, simply return it within 30 days of receiving it and owe nothing.

Title	Price*	Quantity	Total
The Principal As Staff Developer	$16.95		
Beyond Piecemeal Improvements	$21.95		
Cooperative Classroom	$19.95		
Creating Learning Communities: The Role of the Teacher in the 21st Century	$18.95		
Creating the New American School	$19.95		
How Can We Create Thinkers? Questioning Strategies that Work	$22.95		
How Smart Schools Get and Keep Community Support	$19.95		
Leading Schools to Quality (video and leader's guide)	$250.00		
Parents Assuring Student Success	$21.95		
Reconnecting Youth: A Peer Group Approach to Building Life Skills	$139.00		
School Based Management	$21.95		
Sharing Thinking Strategies	$22.95		
Teaching Students to Think	$21.95		
Shipping & Handling: Please add 7% of order total, or a minimum of $3.00, if check or credit card information is not enclosed.			

*Prices subject to change.   TOTAL _____

❏ Check enclosed with order   ❏ Please bill me (P.O. #_____)
❏ VISA or MasterCard   ❏ Money Order

Credit Card No._____ Exp. Date _____
Cardholder Signature _____

SHIP TO:
Name_____ Title _____
Organization _____
Address _____
City_____ State_____ ZIP _____
Phone_____ FAX _____

MAIL TO:
National Educational Service
1252 Loesch Road
Bloomington, IN 47404